# Spy Planes
## and Other Reconnaissance Aircraft

Anthony M. Thornborough

ARMS AND
ARMOUR

---

**Front cover illustration:** 'Sh** hot' over Edwards, California. Now in storage at Beale, and NASA Ames to the North, these titanium metal spyplanes represented the leading edge of airborne reconnaissance. See page 50. [*Lockheed Aeronautical Systems Company*]

**Back cover illustration:** 'Vanilla' Mirage F 1s, including those of the Iraqi air force, are capable of sporting strap-on recce pods such as the Dassault COR-2 slung under this sleek aircraft. The latest pod to be fielded is the Thomson-CSF ASTAC Elint receiver. See page 23. [*Dassault Aviaplans*]

---

# CONTENTS

# INTRODUCTION

Inter-service rivalry exists within the nations of all armed forces. Air arms, in particular, are often singled out by their seafaring and earthbound peers as being an expensive appendage which draws a disproportionate amount of available defence money. But nowhere in war or times of tension does this friendly rivalry melt more rapidly into open-armed co-operation than in the field of reconnaissance. Bombers never get any credit; fighter pilots are dismissed as 'glory boys' despite their work 'behind the scenes'; airlifters enjoy a brief joyful acknowledgment when they fly in the beer alongside the arms, food and medical supplies; close air supporters get a cheer when they drop the bombs on the *right* co-ordinates; but the feats of the recce people seldom go unnoticed for long, especially by the senior commanders on the ground. There is nothing soldiers hate more than the unknown, and nothing better than good quality intelligence which gives them that vital edge, known to today's mobile units as the 'force-multiplying' effect.

International rivalry has also given the necessary impetus for the establishment of sizeable aerial reconnaissance organizations, much of it strategic and clandestine in nature, as wealthy nations eye-up each other's capabilities and weaknesses. Treated as 'spies' at the best of times, unarmed and exposed at the worst, and frequently the butt of political warring, the people who take to the skies on a daily basis to fly these tasks must be at the top of their profession: at one with their machine and its 'snooping' apparatus (ironically, sometimes activated by remote control by ground-based specialists enjoying the comparative luxury of a bunker), and not least of all with the political ramifications and intrinsic

**Arms and Armour Press**
A Cassell Imprint
Villiers House, 41–47 Strand, London WC2N 5JE.

Distributed in the USA by Sterling Publishing Co. Inc., 387 Park Avenue South, New York, NY 10016-8810.

Distributed in Australia by Capricorn Link (Australia) Pty. Ltd, P.O. Box 665, Lane Cove, New South Wales 2066.

hazards of misjudging their flight plans. As crews flying the much-vaunted Mach 3+ SR-71A 'Habu' adjacent to foreign borders used to joke, 'When you are flying at the speed of a high-velocity bullet, you're just twenty seconds away from being shot at and ten seconds away from a major international incident!'. American spyplanes are still treated as 'game' even when they wheel their circuitous reconnaissance 'loops' well outside the boundaries of Cuban or North Korean airspace.

In the 1990s, in Europe at least, we are witnessing the rebirth of an 'Open Skies' policy. START and the Conventional Forces in Europe Treaty are giving rise to the notion that foreign air arms should be permitted to ingress hitherto sacrosanct airspace with a suitably vetted reconnaissance fit to verify compliance with the numerous agreements. This new epoch is spawning a number of new, cheap and comparatively vulnerable reconnaissance 'platforms'. Indeed, only a year ago, the USAF terminated the SR-71 programme in favour of more one-shot satellites, while the USSR similarly has begun to dismantle its sizeable force of high-speed, stratosphere-skimming MiG-25R 'Foxbats' from front-line strategic service, also in favour of the celestial observers. However, recent events in the Persian Gulf have proved that reconnaissance aircraft are a vital standby tool which must not be squandered in favour of short-term political budget-balancing tricks – far better to mothball easily reactivated fighters than be left with a gaping hole in intelligence resources!

This study gives a brief insight into the multitude of aircraft which perform the role of aerial 'spy'. In the new era of economy many of these perform a 'swing-role' function, so the author has avoided the easy trap of dividing the types into 'strategic' or 'tactical', 'maritime' or 'overland', as many of the types covered in this book are adept at all these demanding tasks. Also, emphasis has been placed on those aircraft which are at present, or have recently been, engaged in active reconnaissance duties at key trouble spots, especially over the Persian Gulf, and those which can come within the sharp gaze of a camera lens – never an easy task when one is dealing with highly classified 'spyplanes'.

## Acknowledgments

Many people supplied photos and information for this book and the author extends his sincere thanks to them all, including: Ken Carson, Roger Chesneau, Dale Donovan, John Harty, Tim Laming (and his numerous colleagues across the world, including Scott Van Aken, Christian Gerard, Paul Hoehn and Guiseppe Fassari), Alec J. Molton of *Mil-Slides*, Lois Lovislo and Peter E. Kirkup, Frank B. Mormillo, Eric Schulzinger and Denny Lombard, David Robinson, Wally Rouse, and John Whittenbury. Considerable thanks are due also to the organizations behind many of these names, including: British Aerospace Warton, Dassault-Breguet, The Grumman History Center, Linewrights, Lockheed Aeronautical Systems Company, NASA, HQ RAF Strike Command, Teledyne-Ryan Aeronautical, DAG Publications Ltd; and the publisher Rod Dymott at Arms & Armour Press, whose patience was much appreciated.

Anthony M. Thornborough

Designed and edited by DAG Publications Ltd. Designed by David Gibbons; edited by David Dorrell; layout by Anthony A. Evans; typeset by Ronset Typesetters, Darwen, Lancashire; printed and bound in Spain by Graficromo.

British Library Cataloguing in Publication Data
Thornborough, Anthony M.
Spy planes.
1. Military aircraft
I. Title
623.7467
ISBN 1-85409-096-8

# TECHNIQUES

Aerial reconnaissance encompasses a broad spectrum of intelligence-gathering techniques which range from the 'Mark One Eyeball' to sophisticated electro-magnetic sensors which pick up distant signals on the skywaves. All share an equally valid place in the complex world in which we live. However, it should be noted that the range at which these devices operate, and the time of day at which they are most effective, is subject to a number of variables: weather, latitude (the inclination of the sun playing a major card when it comes to the effectiveness of optical systems), the transmission power of radars, the sensitivity and sophistication of receivers, the focal length of cameras, and a host of other mind-boggling factors, such as interference from the cosmos!

Furthermore, in order to make any valid contribution, reconnaissance products must be 'timely'. Balancing the variables to produce the best quality intelligence material, be it transmitted in 'near real-time' or committed to celluloid or magnetic tape for post-mission analysis (a concept which is fading rapidly into obsolescence), is an art which few appreciate in all its intricacies. On their return from a mission, 'spy-plane' crews seldom have the opportunity to throw the flight plan into the nearest bin and head for the bar! De-briefing is customarily a long, tedious process where crews learn the finer points of their art, and add vital footnotes to the 'hard' and 'soft' copy data.

Despite the complexity of the subject matter, it is possible to reduce the multitude of sensors down to a number of 'core' techniques. Of the many acronyms and terms used, the following are proffered in explanation:

| | |
|---|---|
| AAR | Air-to-air refuelling. |
| AEW | Airborne Early Warning aircraft or radar. |
| AVTR | Airborne Video Tape Recorder, which records imagery in a digital format on magnetic tape for subsequent replay. The latest types permit in-flight editing. |
| AWACS | Airborne Warning & Control System. An AEW aircraft which also provides aerial command functions. |
| CCD | Charged Coupled Device, capable of turning camera pictures into digitalized transmissions for decoding into images back on the ground. CCDs are most often associated with 'real-time' cameras, whose imagery like *FLIR*, can be recorded on *AVTR* or transmitted for near-instant reply elsewhere. |
| Comint | Communications intelligence receiver typically designed to listen in on verbal communications, but sometimes *Telint* data and other low-frequency information connected with test work. |
| ECM | Electronic Countermeasures, a device designed *actively* to disrupt enemy communications or radars. ECCM is a measure designed to reduce susceptibility to ECM. |
| Elint | Electronic intelligence receiver, typically |

◀ RF-104G Starfighters equip the Italian 28° and 132° Gruppi of the 3° Stormo at Villafranca. The Orpheus recce pod is one of their trademarks. Six RF-104Gs from the unit deployed to Turkey on 10 January 1991 as part of the Allied Command Europe Mobile Force's contribution to 'Desert Shield'.

▲ The latest UAV to emerge from the Teledyne Ryan Aeronautical stable is the Model 234. It is depicted here in its ground-launched configuration. Airborne launch trials are being performed from a civil-registered F-4D Phantom II provided by Avtel Flight Test Incorporated. [*Teledyne Ryan Aeronautical*]

▶ Colour infra-red photos such as this frame of Burley, Colorado, are used to assist with land management. [*NASA*]

▲Dedicated reconnaissance aircraft are a luxury which only wealthy nations can afford. This weapons bay, replete with KS-87 framing and KA-56/93 panoramic cameras plus IRLS, belongs to General Dynamics RF-111C A8-143, one of four 'Photo-Pigs' assigned to No 6 Squadron at RAAF Brisbane. [*RAAF*]

◄Electro-optical sensors are replacing traditional cameras in the low-level environment. Most of today's modern front-line fighters feature FLIR, which is used for navigation by night and which can be recorded on tape for post-mission analysis. This Dassault FLIR pod equips a Mirage 2000. [*Avions Marcel Dassault-Breguet Aviation*]

aimed at the higher end of the *RF* spectrum, where radars operate.

**ESM** Electronic Support Measures, typically *Comint* or *Elint* apparatus which passively listens to enemy radar signals. Another term for *Elint,* but usually one which infers subsequent *ECM* or other active measures.

**FAC** Forward Air Controller.

**FLIR** Forward-looking infra-red which looks for a hot-on-cold contrast to produce a monochrome-type TV image. Most FLIRs are in fact slewable, just like an eye, and so may be referred to as Infra-red Detection Sets, as *forwards* may not be a limiting factor! Others are sideways- or downwards-looking (SLIR and DLIR, respectively).

**IDS** Infra-red Detection Set. See *FLIR*.

**IRLS** Infra-red linescan, which records still optical images line-by-line, working much like a *FLIR*, but with significantly greater resolution.

**LOROPS** Long-range optical cameras, typically of 66in focal length or more.

**MAD** Magnetic Anomaly Detector, used to locate submarines.

**Oblique** Side-looking camera which typically 'shoots' a series of frames at 90° to the aircraft's flight path.

**Panoramic** A wide-open perspective, usually a vertical camera which can take horizon-to-horizon shots.

**Real-time** Reconnaissance images or other information which is transmitted back to a ground decoding station within 15 minutes

of its collection in the air – hence the term 'Near Real Time'.

**RF** Radio Frequency, part of the spectrum in which radios, radars and other such equipment operate.

**RPV** Remotely Piloted (unmanned) Vehicle. Known nowadays as UAV.

**RWR** Radar Warning Receiver, commonly associated with self-defence only. These devices, which pick up active enemy radar defences, are becoming increasingly associated with *Elint* functions.

**SAC** Strategic Air Command, USAF.

**SAR** Synthetic Aperture Radar, a *SLAR*-category device which can produce photo-like radar images.

**Sigint** An all-embracing term which encapsulates various modes of passive electronic signal-gathering intelligence, including *Comint, Elint, Telint* and *Urint.*

**SLAR** Sideways-Looking Airborne Radar-mapper.

**Telint** Telemetry intelligence. This is customarily used for gathering information on foreign nations' rocketry and related flight-test work.

**UAV** Unmanned Air Vehicle, the modern term for RPVs.

**Urint** Unintentionally radiated intelligence, including the signals generated through day-to-day training with radars, including unwanted 'sidelobes', and take-off and landing aids plus communications gear, which may be recorded and analyzed for a number of uses.

► The Soviet answer to the U-2: the twin-boomed Molniya (formerly Myasishchyev) Design Bureau M-17 Mystic'. CCCP-17103, wearing Aeroflot logos and residing at the air force museum at Monino, acted as initial high-altitude cruise testbed in the early 'eighties and was followed by at least one further trials machine, tail '17401', which on 28th March 1990 in the hands of Vladimir Arkhipenko attained a height of 71,780ft (a record for a 16–20 metric ton machine). Production of a military twin-engined version is in progress, possessing much improved performance. [*Gabor Szekeres*]

# BRITISH AEROSPACE CANBERRA PR.9/B.2

**Manufacturer:** British Aerospace, Great Britain.
**Users:** RAF, Chile, Germany.
**Role:** General reconnaissance and mapping.
**Data (PR.9):** Length 66ft 8in; wing span 67ft 10in; height 15ft 7in.
**Powerplant:** 2 × Rolls-Royce Avon Mk206 turbojets. Crew 2.

▲The Luftwaffe operates two orange B.2 Canberras which perform earth survey and carto-graphic duties with Erprobungsstelle 61 at Manching.

▶ An RAF hemp-coloured Canberra of No 1 PRU, XH135, in flight. The radar operator sits in a cramped compartment in the nose [*Royal Air Force*]

The majestic Canberra has been embroiled in the world of reconnaissance ever since Roland Beamont took the first of the breed (prototype VN799) into the sky on Friday, 13 May 1949. Today, forty years down the road, RAF Wyton is the home of more than 35 Canberras, split between two operational squadrons, the Operational Conversion Unit – and No 1 Photo Reconnaissance Unit (PRU), the 'spyplane' force. Re-formed at Wyton in June 1982, No 1 PRU operates five PR.9s and its own photo-processing and aircraft engineering facility, permitting it to operate on a worldwide basis as an independent force.

The PR.9 enjoyed a production run of 23 aircraft at Shorts at Belfast and is considered to be the 'hottest' of all Canberras, such being the result of its more powerful Avon 206 turbojets, fighter-style 'bubble' cockpit and extended wing span, designed for high-altitude flight. Present-day equipment includes up to nine cameras, comprising: the vertical and oblique F96 fitted with lenses of 4 to 48in focal length, the nasal F95s set for forward and sideways frames, and the F49 survey camera. Additional devices include the ARI 5969/3 IRLS and Doppler Type 72 scanners.

It is believed that RAF Canberra PR.9s of No 39 Squadron operated covertly from Punta Arenas in Chile during the 1982 Falklands War under Operation 'Corporate', to monitor Argentine activity over the border. Not long after, three machines were taken out of storage at RAF St. Athan and flown to Chile on 15 October 1982, as part of the joint deal. Two machines remain operational with the Chilean Air Force's Grupo de Aviacion No 2's Escuadrilla de Reconocimento at Los Cerrillos.

The Luftwaffe also remain in the Canberra business with two of three (serials 9934, 9935 and 9936) photo-survey B.2s originally supplied in 1966. These are painted in a conspicuous dayglo gloss orange scheme and are flown by the Military Cartographic Office, Erprobungsstelle 61, based at Manching.

The PR.9 is destined to be last Canberra in service, soldiering on until this venerable aircraft celebrates its fiftieth birthday!

# BRITISH AEROSPACE NIMROD MR.2P/R.1

**Manufacturer: British Aerospace, Great Britain.**
**User: RAF.**
**Roles: Maritime Patrol and Sigint.**
**Data: Length 129ft 1in; wing span (excluding ESM pods) 114ft 10in; height 29ft 9½in.**
**Powerplant: 4 × Rolls-Royce Spey 250 turbofans. Crew 12.**

▲ No 51 Squadron, RAF, operates a trio of R.1P Sigint Nimrods from RAF Wyton. XW665 was snatched on film between sorties from NAS Keflavik, Iceland, in August 1989. The aircraft are at present assigned to RAF Akrotiri, Cyprus, to listen in on Iraqi defences. [*Scott Van Aken*]

▶ The proud face of the mighty Nimrod MR2P, glistening in hemp camouflage. The aircraft carries a formidable array of anti-submarine depth-charges and torpedoes, but in peacetime is more commonly tasked on Search & Rescue duties.

Derived from the de Havilland Comet 4C and taking to the air for the first time in its production configuration on 28 June 1968, the Nimrod enjoyed a production run of 46 machines, all of which were delivered to the RAF. Thirty-one of these were later brought up to the MR.2 configuration, which embraced upgraded electronic support measures/ magnetic anomaly detection (ESM/MAD) gear (the EMI ARI 5980 Searchwater and Marconi AQS 901), radar and computers, plus what one crewman rudely described as 'a shade of turd': a khaki 'Hemp' camouflage finish, now standard for several RAF aircraft types.

The latest kit, which transforms the machine into the MR.2P, has added new communications, prominent Loral 1017A ESM wingtip pods codenamed 'Yellowgate', and an AAR probe for extended range and loiter. Operated by No 42 Squadron and the training unit No 236 OCU at RAF St. Mawgan, Cornwall, and by Nos 120, 201 and 206 Squadrons based at RAF Kinloss, Morayshire, additional assets comprise three R.1s (XW664–666) which were delivered to No 51 Squadron at RAF Wyton and formally commissioned on 10 May 1974. Designated R.1P, these three aircraft are engaged in Sigint work, and are forward-deployed across the globe on numerous 'listening' missions which are otherwise beyond the reach of the Government Communications HQ, Cheltenham, and its earthbound satellite outposts. Their equipment fit remains classified.

The Nimrod fleet's primary duties, manned by 'wet' (sea-dipping sensors) and 'dry' (ESM/MAD and radar) teams, embraces maritime search and rescue and anti-submarine warfare. The force's most recent accomplishment has been the successful monitoring of ship movements in the Persian Gulf, as part of the UN-sanctioned naval blockade of oil tankers attempting to run the gauntlet in and out of Iraqi and Kuwaiti ports. The first Nimrod MR.2 to be assigned to the mission left RAF Kinloss on 12 August 1990 with the detachment commander, Wing Commander Andrew Neil, at the controls. In all, three aircraft are on duty at Seeb, located on the north-east coast of Oman, with additional machines holding up the rear, as required. The R.1Ps are at present forward-deployed to RAF Akrotiri, Cyprus.

# BEECHCRAFT RC-12/RU-21 GUARDRAIL

**Manufacturer: Beech Aircraft Corporation, USA.**
**User: US Army.**
**Role: Battle area Sigint, Urint.**
**Data (RC-12K): Length 43ft 10¾in; wing span 58ft 7in; height 14ft 9½in.**
**Powerplant: 2 × Pratt & Whitney PT6-67 turboprops. Crew 2.**

▲ Sprouting a multiplicity of Sigint antennae is Beechcraft RU-21H 68-18112. This mark is forward-deployed to Ramstein AB, Germany, with the 320th Aerial Surveillance Army Company, and is dedicated to Comint tasks using 'Left Foot' and 'Guardrail' equipment. [*MAP*]

Based on the private business class Beechcraft King Air A90/A100 (RU-21) and Super King Air 200 (RC-12) families, several hundred of which have been acquired from the Wichita-based manufacturer for liaison duties by all three US Services, the Army's Sigint Guardrail derivatives are designed to monitor enemy communications and radars and quietly test new systems against prospective enemy defences during 'provocative overflights'. Tabulating Urint also forms a big part of their operational brief.

The US Army at present operates a mixed fleet of RU-21E/G/H and RC-12D/G/H/K types in both active and Air National Guard units, the leading edge of the force being forward-deployed to Germany at Coleman Barracks, Ramstein, Stuttgart and Wiesbaden. The latest in the series is the RC-12K, equipped with the 'Guardrail Common Sensor'. This is designed to pick up enemy communications *and* electronic emitters, effectively combining the functions of the RV-1D (see Grumman OV/RV-1 Mohawk) along with those of older Guardrail V RU-21H and RC-12D aircraft.

▶ The US Army operates a large force of Beechcraft 'Guardrail' snoopers, all of which sprout a multitude of Sigint aerials and a new coat of matt grey paint. [*Mil-Slides*]

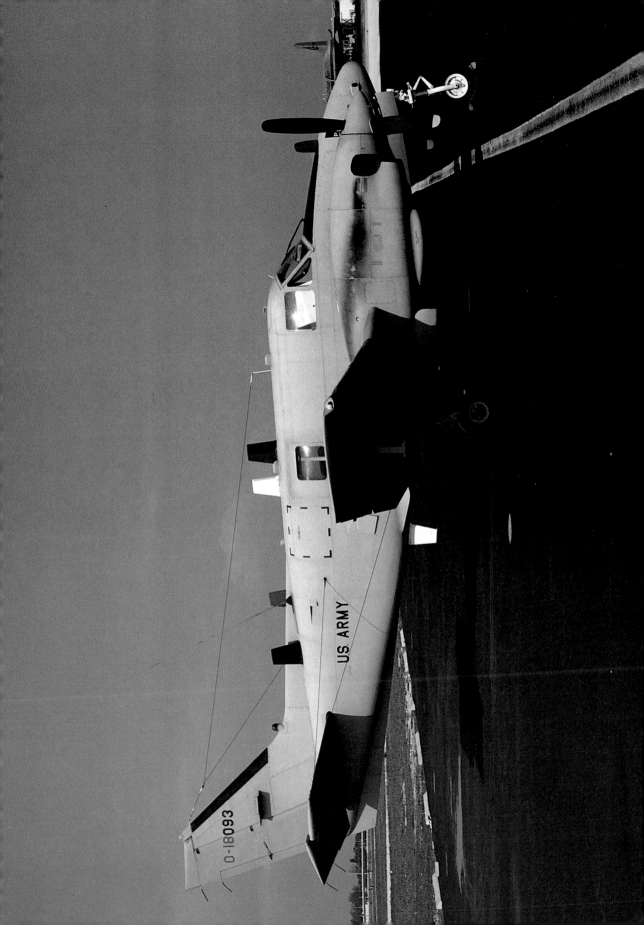

# BOEING RC-135 'FERRET'

**Manufacturer: Boeing Aerospace, USA.**
**User: USAF.**
**Role: Strategic command and control, Sigint.**
**Data: Length 128ft 7⅓in; wing span 130ft 10in; height 41ft 8in.**
**Powerplant: 4 × Pratt & Whitney TF33-P-9 turbofan engines. Crew 12–16.**

Derived from the very successful Boeing KC-135 Stratotanker series, of which no fewer than 732 were built at the company's Seattle, Washington plant, the RC-135 – nicknamed the 'Ferret' because of its Elint 'sniffing' assignment – dates back to the early 1960s when four Model 739-700 aircraft, designated RC-135A, were procured for Photint and Elint duties. These aircraft, long since converted to the 'vanilla' tanker role, paved the way for ten RC-135Bs (Model 739-445B) which have gradually evolved over the past 30 years, in conjunction with further rebuilds from basic C-135B transport stock; so that today's fleet of fourteen surviving aircraft have worked their way right through the alphabet to become RC-135Us (two aircraft operational), RC-135Vs (eight) and RC-135Ws (six active). Serving with the 55th SRW at Offutt AFB, Nebraska, the aircraft employ a number of key forward operating locations, notably RAF Mildenhall, England, Hellenikon in Greece, and Patrick AFB, Florida. Their job is to monitor Warsaw Pact and other potentially hostile air defence electronics so that suitable countermeasures can be prepared for SAC's considerable force of B-52H and B-1B strategic bombers.

Further examples on special Telint and Elint duties include a solitary RC-135X active in Alaska, which is correlating data in support of the Strategic Defense ('Star Wars') initiative under the jurisdiction of the 6th Strategic Wing, along with one TC-135S trainer and two RC-135Ss used for related experimental work. Key sensors include the vintage AN/USD-7 Elint receiver package, which lends the series its unique 'chipmunk' cheeks and 'thimble' nose.

Additional aircraft include the survivors of ten WC-135B weather reconnaissance aircraft stationed at McClellan AFB, California, thirteen (of seventeen) EC-135 'Looking Glass' command posts, and a plethora of NKC-135 trials platforms engaged in various evaluation programmes, ranging from airborne lasers to new cockpit designs, in support of the Air Force Systems Command and the Defense Advanced Research Projects Agency (DARPA).

▲The bulbous growth from this Boeing C-135B houses ALOTS/TRIA space tracking radar originally installed to monitor Apollo space rockets. The aircraft are still engaged with the USAF Air Force Systems Command. [*Mil-Slides*]

▶The USAF's 55th SRW based at Offutt AFB, Nebraska, operates sixteen 'Ferrets' on Elint duties. One of the Wing's RC-135Ws displays its 'chipmunk cheeks' and 'thimble nose', unique to this series. [*Frank B. Mormillo*]

# BOEING E-3 SENTRY

**Manufacturer:** Boeing Aerospace, USA.
**Users:** France, NATO consortium, Saudi Arabia, RAF and USAF.
**Role:** Airborne early warning, command and control.
**Data:** Length 152ft 11in; wing span 145ft 9in; height 41ft 9in.
**Powerplant:** 4 × Pratt & Whitney TF33 (E-3A/B/C and E-8A) or SNECMA/GE CFM56
(E-3D/F, KE-3A and E-6A) turbofans. Crew 23.

The 100-ton 'flying radar' was evolved from a pair of EC-137D Airborne Warning &
Control System (AWACS) testbeds, the first of which flew on 5 February 1972. Based on
the Boeing 707-320C airliner, production started with 24 of the 'Core' E-3A mark, which
were formed under the 552nd AWAC Wing based at Tinker AFB, Oklahoma, beginning
on 24 March 1977. Equipped with the distinctive Westinghouse AN/APY-1 rotodome and
IBM CC-1 computer processing system, the E-3A Sentry plots, interrogates and maps all
aircraft within its scan and projects the synthesized data on nine SDCs (Situation Display
Consoles) and two ADUs (Auxiliary Display Units). The crew then vector friendly fighter
aircraft on to hostile targets.

The radar works in a number of modes, including passive detection, full-power beyond-
the-horizon scan, and shorter-range pulse-Doppler non-elevation or elevation scan. A
second batch of sixteen 'Standard' E-3As introduced a maritime tracking facility and a
combined pulse repetition frequency output scanning mode for the simultaneous tracking
of ships and aircraft. Aircraft Nos 25–34 have since been upgraded to E-3C standard with
five extra SDCs and jam-resistant communications, while the original 24 aircraft have
been retrofitted with new CC-2 computers and most of the other features of the E-3C to
bring them up to the E-3B configuration. The 34 aircraft equip the component squadrons
of the 552nd AWAC Wing (the 963rd, 964th, and 965th AWACS and the 966th AWAC
Training Squadron) in Oklahoma, and also maintain permanent detachments at NAS
Keflavik, Iceland, Kadena AB, Okinawa, and Elmendorf AFB, Alaska.

NATO was the second biggest customer, with an order for eighteen aircraft. These are
registered in Luxembourg (serials LX-N90442 to LX-N90459) and wear the coat of arms
of the Grand Duchy on their tails. The machines are headquartered at Geilenkirchen,
Germany. Britain placed an order for seven E-3D aircraft (ZH101-ZH107) to replace its
obsolete Shackletons and fill the void left by the aborted AEW Nimrod venture; these are
now being delivered. The Sentry Training Squadron (STS) was formed at RAF

▲The Westinghouse
AN/APY-1 radar (since
updated to APY-2
standard) scans through
complete circle every ten
seconds. It features
resilience to enemy
jamming and has
advanced IFF
(identification friend or
foe interrogation)
capabilities, but it may be
vulnerable to enemy
fighters unless operating
at a considerable distance
from the forward battle
area. [*Boeing*]

▲▶The RAF has ordered
seven E-3D Sentries and
these will equip No 8
Squadron at RAF
Waddington. The
machines feature a probe
for AAR, and the modern
fuel-efficient SNECMA/
General Electric CFM56
turbofan engines. [*Royal
Air Force*]

▶Grumman's Melbourne
Florida division is
developing the E-8A
Joint-STARS. Under
project 'Deep Strike' the
testbed flew to Europe
during 1990 for
operational evaluation.
The machine operated
principally from RAF

Mildenhall to Suffolk, England, and Geilenkirchen Air Base, Germany. [*Grumman Corporation*]

Waddington on 1 June 1990, and the force will achieve operational status on 30 June 1991 when No 8 Squadron moves to RAF Lossiemouth. France's Armée de l'Air has four E-3Fs on order, the first of which arrived at Le Bourget, near Paris, in November 1990, while five KE-3As with an AAR drogue capability have been built for Saudi Arabia. Japan is considering the acquisition of four E-3J aircraft in its next five-year defence plan.

Other Boeing 707 derivatives abound. Among the more significant are 24 E-6 TACAMOs (Take Charge And Move Out), employed for US Navy submarine command and control functions, and the USAF developmental E-8 J-STARS (Joint Surveillance Target Attack Radar System), developed by Grumman, which uses SAR to plot the positions of fixed and moving enemy armoured forces, and then directs strike aircraft. The USAF is seeking 22 E-8A conversions, to be operated by joint Army and Air Force crews.

# DASSAULT-BREGUET ATL2 ATLANTIQUE

**Manufacturer: Avions Marcel Dassault-Breguet Aviation, France.**
**User: France.**
**Role: Maritime patrol, anti-shipping and ASW.**
**Data: Length 107ft ⅔in; wing span (including ESM pods) 122ft 9in; height 35ft 8¾in.**
**Powerplant: 2 × Rolls-Royce Tyne 21 turboprops. Crew 24.**

▲ ▶The majestic Dassault Breguet ATL2 Atlantique in flight. Mission endurance is typically eight hours, operating at a tactical radius of 1,000nm. [*Avions Marcel Dassault-Breguet Aviation*]

▶The ATL2's capacious rear cabin. From left to right are the ESM/ECM/MAD station, TACCO/radar consoles (round displays), and acoustic desks (rectangular displays). [*Avions Marcel Dassault-Breguet Aviation*]

The ancestor of the modern ATL2 is the Br 1150 Atlantique which won a NATO competition held in 1958 for an ASW and maritime patrol aircraft; there were no fewer than 27 separate contenders. The winner was subsequently produced by a consortium bearing the acronym SEBCAT, furnishing a total of 87 aircraft: 40 for France's Aéronavale (three of which were later sold to Pakistan), 20 for Germany's Marineflieger (of which a handful serving with Group 3 at Nordholz have since assumed a dedicated Sigint role), nine for the Dutch Marine Luchtvaartdienst, and eighteen for Italy's Marinavia. The passing of time and need for newer technology led to the development of the Atlantique Nouvelle Génération, referred to simply as the ATL2, which first flew in May 1981. France has a requirement for 42 aircraft and firm orders already exist for nineteen ATL2s.

The ATL2's cabin is divided into five stations: the two-man cockpit; the solitary navigation-communication desk; the ESM/ECM/MAD consoles (the heart of the aircraft); the TACCO (tactical co-ordination)/radar stations; and the dual acoustic posts. The sensors themselves range from a simple nose-mounted OMERA 35 camera (fitted with lenses of 3in to 12in focal length) to the Crouzet MAD receiver in the tail. In between these two extremities, the aircraft packs a SAT/TRT FLIR turret to cut through haze and darkness, 100 disposable sonobuoys, and the Thomson-CSF ARAR-13 ESM Elint receiver. The weapons bay, designed to despatch submarines or ships, sew mines or drop a rescue kit with Mk 46 torpedoes or a pair of deadly AM39 Exocets, is backed up by underwing pylons which can pack a hefty load of up to four Matra Magic heat-seeking missiles for self-defence. It is a formidable machine by anyone's reckoning.

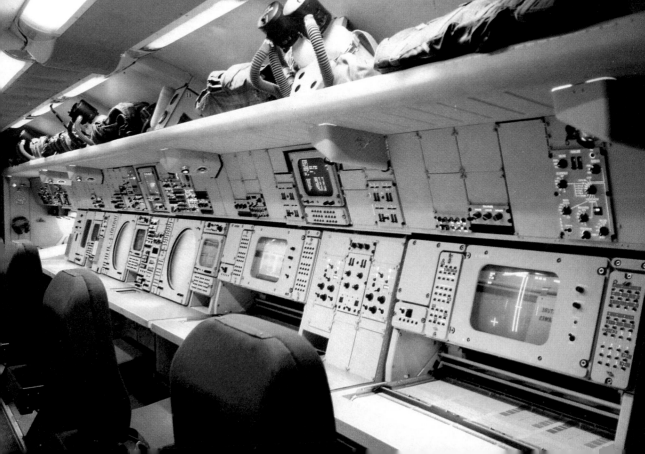

# DASSAULT-BREGUET MIRAGE III/IV/5R

**Manufacturer:** Avions Marcel Dassault-Breguet Aviation, France.
**Users:** Abu Dhabi, Belgium, Colombia, France, Libya, Pakistan, Switzerland and South Africa.
**Role:** Tactical reconnaissance/strike.
**Data (5R):** Length 51ft; wing span 26ft 11½in; height 14ft 9in.
**Powerplant:** 1 × SNECMA Atar 9C afterburning turbojet. Crew 1.

A grand total of 1,422 of the famous Mirage III/5 series was manufactured by Dassault-Breguet following the successful development of a sub-scale interceptor which first flew in 1955. Entering service with France's Armée de L'Air six years later, and gaining fame in the hands of Israel's Chey'l Ha'Avir during the lightning six-day war of 1967, the manufacturers were quick to capitalize on the rapidly growing order books and have continued to develop reconnaissance derivatives. First in the series was the Mirage IIIR, which first flew on 31 October 1961, equipped with OMERA Type 31 cameras and CSF radar altimeter. France procured fifty for its own armed forces and these were progressively updated with Type 33 and 40 sensors, and SAT Cyclope IRLS. This equipment has also formed the basis of most overseas customer suites, although Belgium and Pakistan employ British Vinten cameras. Production of all marks in the 'family' closed at 159 aircraft.

Many nations fly the Mirage IIIR and 5R as direct sales or as hand-me-down operators as the aircraft carry a high price in the second-hand arms market. Among the biggest users are Pakistan (thirteen Doppler-equipped IIIRPs, assigned to No 20 Squadron at Rafiqui), South Africa (four IIIRZs and four IIIR2Zs with uprated Atar 9K50 engines), and Switzerland (eighteen IIIRSs assigned to Fliegerstaffel 10 at Dübendorf, built under licence by the Swiss Federal Aircraft Factory at Emmen). Of the 5R operators, Belgium ranks top with 27 Mirage 5BRs assembled by SABCA (eighteen remaining, assigned to the 42nd 'Mephisto' Squadron, 3rd Wing, at Bierset and destined to remain in service until 1993), followed by Abu Dhabi (three 5RADs based at Maquatra), Colombia (two 5CORs under Grupo Aereo de Combate 1 at German Olano), and Libya (ten 5DRs at Gemal Abdel Nasser air base).

Mention should be made of one other delta-winged Mirage, the twin-engined IVA, of which 62 were built for France's nuclear arm, the Force de Frappe. Thirty of the updated IVPs remain in front-line service, including a dozen aircraft assigned to Escadron 1/328 'Aquitaine' at Bordeaux-Mérignac, the chief Centre d'Instruction des Forces Aériennes Strategiques, on long-range reconnaissance and training duties. Four of the aircraft carry CT52 sensor pods toting OMERA type 35 and 36 cameras and SAT Super Cyclope IRLS.

▲Belgium's 42nd 'Mephisto' Squadron celebrated 75 years of history with this fiery-looking Mirage 5BR. The unit operates eighteen recce Mirages from Bierset, and on 10 January 1991 committed the force to Turkey in support of NATO's efforts in the Gulf. [*Tim Laming*]

▲▶France's Armée de L'Air only recently relinquished the last of its Mirage IIIRs. This example is one of a series painted in special schemes. [*Fritz Becker*]

▶The Swiss built eighteen Mirage IIIRSs under licence at Emmen, and these operate with Fliegerstaffel 10 at Dübendorf. [*Paul Hoehn*]

▶▶The business end of the Mirage 5R, with its Vinten cameras exposed to sunlight. All but the Belgian and Pakistani Mirages are equipped with OMERA cameras. [*Tim Laming*]

# DASSAULT-BREGUET MIRAGE F 1CR

Manufacturer: Avions Marcel Dassault-Breguet Aviation, France.
User: France.
Role: Tactical reconnaissance/strike.
Data: Length 50ft 2½in; wing span 30ft; height 14ft 9in.
Powerplant: 1 × SNECMA Atar 9K50 afterburning turbojet. Crew 1.

▲Several Armée de L'Air Mirage F 1CRs have adopted this desert scheme, originally designed for operations in Chad but equally useful for the Gulf. [*Avions Marcel Dassault-Breguet Aviation*]

France's Armée de L'Air is the exclusive operator of the dedicated F 1CR-200. Including the two prototypes (Nos 601 and 602), the first of which flew on 20 November 1981, no fewer than 64 were procured and deployed with the 33e Escadre based at Base Aérienne 124, Strasbourg-Entzeim, under three Escadrons de Reconnaissance: 1/33 'Belfort', 2/33 'Savoie', and 3/33 'Melles'.

The sensor equipment is integrated with the central SNAR navigation computer, Uliss 47 INS, and Cyrano IV-MR ground-mapping radar and includes a variety of internally mounted devices, such as the OMERA-33 vertical and -40 panoramic cameras, and the aptly named Super Cyclope WCM 2400 IRLS (which replaced the starboard gun). These combine to provide all-weather, round-the-clock capability, while reconnaissance products may be data-linked to ground commanders via the Système Aérotransportable de Reconnaissance Aérienne (SARA), which embraces up to nine portable shelters complete with provision for NBC protection.

**Manufacturer: Avions Marcel Dassault-Breguet Aviation, France.**
**User: France.**
**Role: Fleet reconnaissance and aerial refuelling.**
**Data: Length 47ft 8in; wing span 31ft 6in; height 142ft 2in.**
**Powerplant: 1 × SNECMA Atar 8B turbojet. Crew 1.**

The first of seven development fighter versions of the Etendard flew on 24 July 1956, to be followed by a production run of 69 machines between 1961 and 1964, all for France's Aéronavale. Close on the heels of these came 21 of the unarmed IVP reconnaissance Etendards, equipped with nose-mounted OMERA cameras. While the bulk of the surviving force of IVM fighters has been supplanted by the nuclear- and Exocet missile-capable Super Etendard, a dozen IVP machines remain in service with Flottille 16F, land-based between cruises aboard the aircraft-carrier *Clemenceau* at Landivisiau. The unit performs a secondary 'buddy' aerial refuelling task.

# FAIRCHILD-REPUBLIC OA-10A THUNDERBOLT II

**Manufacturer: Fairchild-Republic, USA.**
**User: USAF.**
**Role: Close Air Support and Forward Air Control.**
**Data: Length 53ft 4in; wing span 57ft 6in; height 14ft 8in.**
**Powerplant: 2 × General Electric T34-GE-100A turbofans. Crew 1.**

▲ The USAF's 57th Fighter Weapons Wing evaluates combat tactics operationally for Tactical Air Command. This aggressive-looking 'Warthog' was one of the first to sport the deflector gun muzzle, which overcame a problem with cartridge residue build-up from the GAU-8/A Avenger. [*Patrick Martin*]

Designed as a CAS machine tasked with the specific job of destroying enemy armour with its huge GAU-8/A 30mm Avenger 'Gatling' gun, packing 1,350 rounds of high-explosive or armour-piercing ammunition, the now defunct Republic Aviation Company's A-10A – known affectionately to its crews as the 'Warthog' – is increasingly being devoted to the FAC observation role, ousting aged OA-37s and OV-10s from the USAF inventory. The A-10A is dogged by a poor top speed (300kt in the battle configuration) and its CAS duties are to be taken over by 300–400 Block 30 General Dynamics F-16 Fighting Falcons adapted to the A-16 attack role, from Fiscal Year 1995.

The prototype 'Warthog' first flew on 10 May 1972 with Howard 'Sam' Nelson at the controls. Production at Hagerstown, Maryland, totalled 713 A-10As, including one two-seat FLIR-equipped Night/Adverse Weather A-10B conversion (31664), which made its first flight in May 1979. Production deliveries started on 5 November 1975, and by the time production had ceased nine years later, the type had equipped seventeen active squadrons and ten reserve units. Current plans call for the adaptation of 220 machines to the full OA-10A observation standard, combining the existing Pave Penny passive laser tracker, LN-39 INS and Avenger gun with a new FLIR (of which three types are presently under evaluation), a new GEC wide-angle Head-Up Display, and the Rockwell-Collins CP-1516/ASQ automatic target hand-off system which will relay target co-ordinates over secure radio links to friendly strike aircraft.

One of the premier units to form with the 'basic' machine in the OA-10A FAC role was the 23rd Tactical Air Support Squadron based at Davis-Monthan AFB, Arizona. The squadron deployed to Saudi Arabia on 24 November 1990. The FAC task is straight-forward but demands considerable courage. Once spotted visually or via a laser return from a portable infantry designator, the target may be marked with a burst of gunfire or rockets. Friendly support aircraft are then provided with target co-ordinates and headings. The 'all-up' OA-10 mark equipped with FLIR and the CP-1516/ASQ for greater automation and all-weather capability will become available during 1992.

▲▲ Once the proud mount of the Italian 'Frecce Tricolori' aerobatic display team, the G-91 and its recce-trainer twin-seat companion now serve as trainers and target tugs. [*Tim Laming*]

▲ Italy's Regia Aero-nautica maintains a nominal force of G-91Rs at San Angelo. [*Giuseppe Fassari*]

**Manufacturer: Aeritalia SpA (formerly Fiat SpA), and under licence in Germany by MBB, VFW-Fokker and Dornier.**
**Users: Germany, Italy and Portugal.**
**Role: Tactical reconnaissance, strike, training.**
**Data: Length 33ft 9¼in; wing span 28ft 1in; height 13ft 1½in.**
**Powerplant: 1 × Rolls-Royce Orpheus 80302 turbojet. Crew 1.**

Now nearing extinction, the nimble Fiat G-91R serves in limited numbers in Continental Europe with the armed forces of Germany, Italy and Portugal. The Luftwaffe operates a handful of G-91R/3s which have been modified by Condor Flugdienst for target-towing duties. Italy's Aeronautica Militare flies a token force under the 14° Gruppo based at San Angelo, while Portugal continues to operate the survivors of 25 ex-German machines with Esquadra 301 at Montijo (further examples based on the Azores having recently been withdrawn from service). All machines are destined to be retired shortly, owing to poor availability rates exacerbated by the age of the aircraft; however, the G-91 remains popular with its pilots and instructors and is considered to be a 'fun' aircraft to fly.

# GENERAL DYNAMICS RF-111C AARDVARK

**Manufacturer: General Dynamics, USA.**
**User: RAAF.**
**Role: Tactical and Maritime reconnaissance, strike.**
**Data: Length 73ft 6in; wing span, extended 70ft, swept 33ft 11in; height 17ft ½in.**
**Powerplant: 2 × Pratt & Whitney TF30-P-103 augmented turbofans. Crew 2.**

Derived from the Tactical Fighter Experimental (TFX) which first flew on 24 December 1964, the RF-111C is arguably the most capable reconnaissance aircraft operational in the Pacific. Of the two dozen F-111Cs built for the Royal Australian Air Force and delivered, somewhat belatedly, in 1973, four (serials A8-126, -134, -143 and -146) were adapted in 1979 to the reconnaissance mission and serve exclusively with No 6 Sqn at RAAF Amberley, near Brisbane.

The equipment fit has much in common with that used by the McAir RF-4C/E 'Photo Phantom', but the Australian aircraft offers substantially improved range, fully automatic terrain-following flight, and significant weapons capability as part of its 'swing-role' assignment. The sensors are strapped to a pallet adapted from the aircraft's internal weapons bay and comprise: KA-56E low-altitude and KA-94A4 high-altitude panoramic cameras, a pair of CAI KS-87C semi-oblique framing cameras, a Honeywell AAD-5 IRLS, and an electro-optical viewfinder linked to an AVTR. The aircraft's General Electric APQ-110 attack radar serves the secondary role of all-weather mapper, particularly useful for maritime work.

The RF-111C provides both strategic and tactical reconnaissance products, depending on the nature of the tasking, in concert with back-up, mobile, tent-based interpretation teams which permit operations from austere operating locations. Because of its talents, the aircraft's responsibilities embrace not only the entire Australian continent and New Zealand, but extend as far west as the Indian Ocean, and north beyond the Timor Sea to Indonesia and Malaysia. In common with the remainder of the 'Aardvark' fleet, the RF-111Cs are about to undergo a digital avionics update which will extend their useful life to the year 2010.

▲ The RF-111C retains a full attack capability, but all weapons must be carried externally, the bomb bay having been given over to Photint equipment. Modifications to the cockpit included a reconnaissance control panel on the right-hand console, and an electro-optical TV viewfinder left of the huge radar scope hood. [*RAAF*]

▶ The 'Aussies' get out and about a great deal on manoeuvres, and recent venues have included Nellis, Nevada, for 'Red Flag' exercises, and Bergstrom, Texas, for the competitive Reconnaissance Air Meet. One of its quartet of RF-111Cs soaks up the American sun, complete with tarpaulin to protect the sensitive static pressure sensors and radar kit. [*Mil-Slides*]

# GRUMMAN EA-6B PROWLER

**Manufacturer: Grumman Corporation, USA.**
**User: US Navy.**
**Role: Tactical jamming and Sigint.**
**Data: Length 59ft 10in; wing span 53ft; height 16ft 3in.**
**Powerplant: 2 × Pratt & Whitney TF52-P-408 turbojets. Crew 4.**

At the time of writing, 121 EA-6Bs out of a grand total of 170 produced were operational with the Fleet. The pugnacious Prowler was developed as a stretched electronic warfare version of the Grumman A-6 Intruder, and made its maiden flight on 28 May 1968 with test pilot Don King at the stick. Its most distinctive feature is the fin-top 'football', housing the receivers for the Eaton AIL AN/ALQ-99 receivers which monitor enemy radar activity. Processed and displayed to two Naval Flight Officers in the rear of the 'four-holer', the information may be recorded for Elint purposes, or for the initiation of jamming, conducted by means of up to five interchangeable underwing pods. The Prowler was the first aircraft to introduce 'closed loop', 'look-through' jamming (ie, being able simultaneously to receive enemy signals and jam them), and uses extensive automation. An AN/ALQ-92 communications jammer (comjam), since replaced by the ASQ-191 and due to be superseded by the Sanders AN/ALQ-149, may similarly be used for Comint; and in 1988 the US Navy publicly admitted that it is customary during times of tension for an enlisted Farsi or other language expert to take one of the seats.

The original or basic model first saw action during the fearsome 'Linebacker' bombing of North Vietnam in December 1972. Followed by a series of 'Expanded' (EXCAP) and 'Improved Capability' (ICAP-I and -II) updates to the AN/ALQ-99 jamming package, the aircraft has since seen extensive action in the Middle East, including Libya (April 1986), the Straits of Hormuz (April 1988); while six of the Fleet's fourteen Tactical Electronic Warfare Squadrons ('TECELRONS') are at present on station in the Persian Gulf, leaving only seven active and one training, plus the USMC unit (the 'Playboys') out of the fray.

Work is now under way on the 'Advanced Capability' version, which boasts speedier radar-processing times, expanded radar frequency coverage, new TF52-P-409 engines and aerodynamic refinements to reduce the aircraft's now critical stall margin. These improvements will be retrofitted to the existing force.

▲ ICAP-II Prowler AE605 was assigned to VAQ-132 'Scorpions' aboard the USS *Forrestal* when this photo was taken during 1986. The grey camouflage decor weathers rapidly and constant touch-up work performed by the Plane Captains speeds the process. [*Grumman Corporation*]

▲ ▶ The front station in the EA-6B is occupied by the pilot, responsible for the safety of the aircraft and crew, and the right seat by a qualified navigator tasked also with Comint and Comjam.

▶ Two Electronic Countermeasures Officers (ECMOs) are in charge of the Prowler's receivers and countermeasures, used for 'soft kill' jamming or for passive Elint. [*Grumman Corporation*]

# GRUMMAN EF-111A RAVEN

Manufacturer: Grumman Corporation, USA.
User: USAF.
Role: Tactical jamming and Elint.
Data: Length 74ft; wing span, fully extended (at 16deg) 63ft, fully swept (at 72.5deg) 31ft 11in; height 20ft.
Powerplant: 2 × Pratt & Whitney TF30-P-109 augmented turbofans. Crew 2.

A total of 42 F-111A aircraft were adapted to the production 'Electronic Fox' configuration by Grumman at the corporation's Calverton facility and delivered to the USAF between 4 November 1981 and 23 December 1985. These land-based aircraft perform a role identical to that handled by the US Navy's EA-6B Prowlers, save for comjam, and are deployed operationally with the 390th Electronic Combat Squadron at Mountain Home AFB, Idaho (which is also responsible for crew training), and the 42nd ECS stationed at RAF Upper Heyford, Oxfordshire, England.

The EF-111A, dubbed the 'Raven' in USAF service, carries only one dedicated electronics specialist – the right-seat Electronic Warfare Officer or 'Crow' – who relies on the significant automation provided by Eaton-AIL's AN/ALQ-99E jamming sub-system. Further to reduce the workload, this is interfaced with the aircraft's self-defence electronics, the Dalmo-Victor AN/ALR-62 Terminal Threat Warning System and Sanders AN/ALQ-137 self-protection jammer, and full pre-flight programming. In common with the Prowler, the Raven performs ESM missions, mapping the EOB of prospective enemies for tactical operations.

The aircraft were first committed to combat during Operation 'El Dorado Canyon', the punitive strike on Libya conducted in April 1986, when a pair of 42nd ECS aircraft (67-052 and -057) performed stand-off jamming. The aircraft's primary duties are to support NATO and America's rapid deployment forces, and operational venues have subsequently included MCAS Iwakuni, Japan, and the Middle East.

The machines have recently undergone an engine modification from TF30-P-103 to -109 standard, boosting total augmented thrust by over two tons to 41,680lb. A digital navigation update is also in progress and, in common with the EA-6B Prowler, the aircraft should soon receive a 'hard kill' capability, including the ability to programme and launch Northrop AGM-136 Tacit Rainbow anti-radar drones. Piloted by some of the USAF's most experienced F-111 'sticks', the Raven has enjoyed a prestigious career and is destined to serve beyond the turn of the century.

▲ Forty-two EF-111A Ravens were converted from bomber stock and equip the 390th ECS 'Wild Boars' at Mountain AFB, Idaho, and the 42nd ECS at RAF Upper Heyford, England. [*Frank B. Mormillo*]

▲▶Raven '052, nick-named 'Cherry Bomb', makes a swift departure. The clean configuration is common to these aircraft.

▶ The Raven is flown by two men and so it features extensive automation. Radar threats are presented on the large Detail Display Indicator at right. [*Grumman Corporation*]

# GRUMMAN F-14A TARPS

▲Tomcats at rest between missions on the deck of the USS *America* comprising aircraft from VF-33 'Starfighters' and VF-102 'Diamondbacks'. [*Mil-Slides*]

**Manufacturer: Grumman/Naval Avionics, USA.**
**User: United States Navy.**
**Data: Length 61ft 2in; wing span, fully extended (at 20deg) 64ft 1½in, fully swept (at 68deg) 38ft 2in; height 16ft.**
**Powerplant: 2 × Pratt & Whitney TF30-P-412A or -414A augmented turbofans. Crew 2.**

Development of the TARPS (Tactical Air Reconnaissance Pod System) was prompted by the wholesale withdrawal of dedicated RA-5C and RF-8G carrier-borne reconnaissance aircraft from the US Navy's inventory during the late 1970s and early 1980s. Rather than procure a follow-on dedicated reconnaissance aircraft, the Navy elected to equip selected numbers of its Grumman F-14A Tomcat Fleet defence fighters with the strap-on TARPs, which is bolted to the starboard aft Phoenix missile station.

Initial development, in co-operation with Grumman, was performed by the Warminster, Pennsylvania-based Naval Air Development Center. The systems were manufactured by the Naval Avionics Center at Indianapolis, Indiana. Line modifications to all 64 F-14As, of which 49 were performed by Grumman and an additional fifteen by NARF Norfolk, Virginia (all of which carry the prefix TARPS next to their Bureau Numbers as an identifying feature), embraced new wiring harnesses and a 'recon control' panel fitted to the left rear cockpit console. In action, the back-seater is the primary sensor manager, although the pilot also has access to a simple manual on/off switch on the control column. In its all-up configuration and with the aircraft systems selected for air-to-ground, the inertial navigation system helps furnish optimum steering commands on the pilot's HUD, and auto-cueing of the podded sensors. *All* the latest F-14D Tomcats now joining the Fleet feature provision for TARPS.

An extra panel was added to the Tomcat's rear left console to permit operation and monitoring of TARPS. 4 F-14As and all F-14Ds are TARPS-capable.

The 1,700lb TARPS pod contains a pair of forward- and downward-looking CAI KS-87B framing cameras, a Fairchild KA-99 low-altitude panoramic camera, and a Honeywell AN/AAD-5A IRLS for day/night visual reconnaissance duties.

The first of 48 production and four refurbished development pods entered operational service with the Fleet in May 1981, when VF-84 'The Jolly Rogers' deployed aboard the USS *Nimitz*. This set a pattern which remains the norm today: each seafaring Carrier Air Wing boasts a complement of two TARPS F-14As – appropriately nicknamed 'Peeping Toms' – and at least three crews trained to use the device. At present operational in the Persian Gulf, the 'Peeping Toms' first saw action with VF-31 'The Tomcatters' aboard the USS *John F. Kennedy* during CVW-3's Mediterranean cruise of 1983–84, where the unit clocked up 39 TARPS missions over the Lebanon. As the Tomcat may still carry a reasonable complement of missiles for self-defence, the TARPS F-14A is undoubtedly not a reconnaissance aircraft to tangle with!

# GRUMMAN E-2C HAWKEYE

**Manufacturer:** Grumman Corporation, USA.
**Users:** US Navy, Egypt, Israel, Japan and Singapore.
**Role:** Airborne Early Warning, drug interdiction and Elint.
**Data:** Length 57ft 6¾in; wing span 80ft 7in; height 18ft 3¾in.
**Powerplant:** 2 × Allison T56-A-415 turboprops. Crew 5.

▲ Japan's Air Self-Defence Force received eight E-2C Hawkeyes and has ordered five more. The aircraft serve with 601 Hikotai at Misawa AB. [*Grumman Corporation*]

▶ The drivers' seats in the Hawkeye. The radar operators sit at consoles in the rear cabin. [*Grumman Corporation*]

The Hawkeye can trace its lineage to 21 October 1960 when the prototype E-2 first took to the sky above Grumman's Bethpage-based 'Iron Works' in Long Island, New York. It is aptly nicknamed the 'eyes and ears' of the US Fleet. Manufacture of three testbeds and 59 production E-2As (of which 52 were brought up to interim E-2B standard and two to the TE-2C trainer configuration) took place between 1964 and 1969. At the time of writing, these had been followed by no fewer than 144 (up to and including BuNo 164112) of the definitive E-2C mark, which first flew on 20 January 1971 and joined the Fleet the following year. This top-of-the-line model is capable of tracking three million cubic miles of airspace during one ten-second scan from its sophisticated AN/APS-125 rotodome, permitting its three specialist radar operators to monitor both shipping and air activity and to vector friendly fighters on to the opposition during times of tension or hostilities. Extensive automation is made possible by means of an Advanced Radar Processing System (ARPS), enabling the simultaneous tracking of up to 250 'bogeys'.

The E-2C Hawkeye has enjoyed a remarkable safety record for a carrier-based aircraft: a mere three losses during 20 years of arduous shipborne missions. At present assigned to two US Naval Reserve Wings, two Fleet training outfits headquartered at NAS Miramar, California, and NAS Norfolk, Virginia, together with thirteen operational AEW squadrons, the Hawkeye's comparatively modest operating costs have generated valuable overseas sales, including: five to Egypt (BuNos 162791-'792 and 162823-'825, delivered during 1987); four to Israel (BuNos 160771-'774, delivered during 1978); four to Singapore (BuNos 162793-'796, delivered during 1986); and thirteen to Japan (eight comprising BuNos 161400-'403 and 161786-'789, delivered starting in 1982, with five more on the order books). The US Navy plans to continue production at six aircraft annually and these machines will incorporate the AN/APS-145 radar which offers superior resilience to enemy countermeasures and improved overland tracking capability.

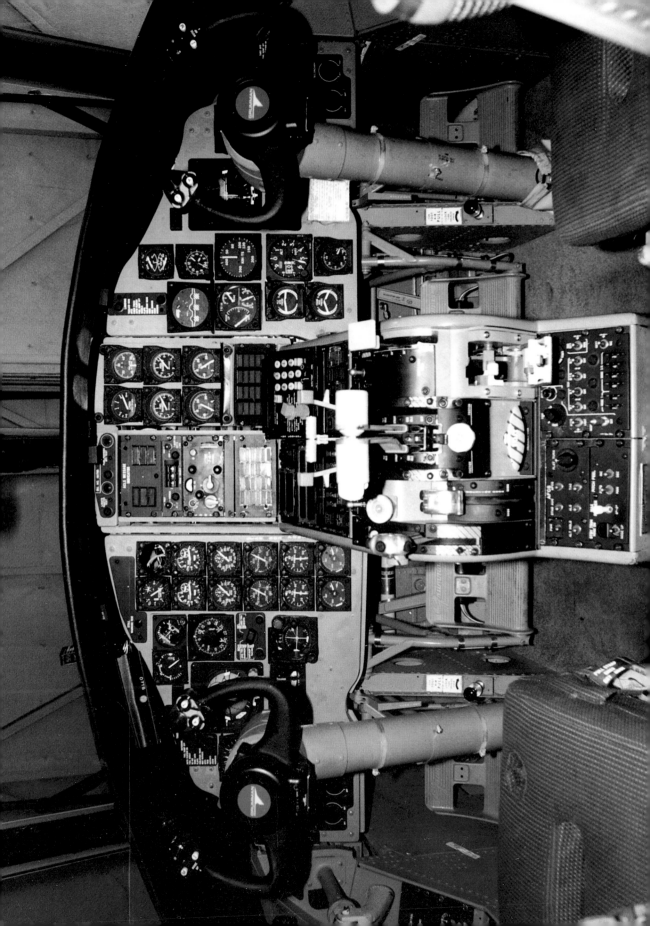

**Manufacturer:** Grumman Corporation, USA.
**Users:** US Army, Israel.
**Role:** Battlefield area reconnaissance and Sigint.
**Data (OV-1D):** Length with SLAR 44ft 11in, without 41ft; wing span 48ft; height 12ft 8in.
**Powerplant:** 2 × Avco Lycoming T53-L-701 turboprops. **Crew 2.**

▲ A three-tailed RV-1D Mohawk sits fat and happy amidst the thick snow at NAS Keflavik, Iceland. These aircraft perform an Elint function using 'Quick Look II' devices. [*Scott Van Aken*]

▶ The OV-1D Mohawk boasts an AN/APS-94F SLAR, plus a pair of panoramic and serial frame cameras. In place of the SLAR a UAS-4 IRLS may be carried. Additional equipment comprises Sanders AN/ALQ-147(V)2 'Hot Brick' infra-red countermeasures, and optional LS-59A photo-flash pods.

The first of nine YOV-1 prototypes flew on 14 April 1959, to be followed by 64 OV-1As equipped with KA-30 and -60 cameras, 101 OV-1Bs which introduced the APS-94A SLAR 'canoe' and a bigger wing extended by 5ft 10½in, and 133 OV-1CS which added 'first-generation' UAS-4 infra-red detection equipment to the basic OV-1A fit. All three models served with distinction in Vietnam, flying round-the-clock operations over the steamy jungles to track Viet Cong and North Vietnamese troop movements. The definitive model is the 'Delta', of which 37 examples were built from new and a further 108 from old stock. At least two of these were supplied to Israel during 1976. The standard fit includes an updated APS-94F SLAR or AAS-24 infra-red scanner, plus a pair of KA-60C panoramic and a KA-76 serial frame cameras. 110 machines are scheduled to remain in service into the next century, and these aircraft are in the process of receiving a Block 1 upgrade which includes a structural revamp, added communications equipment and other avionics compatible with Joint-STARS (see Boeing E-3 AWACS), along with new T53-L-704 engines.

Also in service are 36 electronic 'snoopers' designated the RV-1D 'Quick Look II'. These are equipped with AN/ALQ-133 devices designed to map and analyze enemy ground-based radars.

The cutting edge of the surviving force of Mohawks is forward-deployed to Germany, where the two military intelligence battalions based at Stuttgart and Wiesbaden each operate a mix of a dozen OV-1Ds and six RV-1Ds in concert with Beechcraft Guardrail aircraft (See Beechcraft RC-12/RU-21 Guardrail). A similar clandestine force operates from South Korea, with the remainder assigned to Stateside Army and National Guard units. Beechcraft RC-12K 'Guardrail Common Sensor' aircraft are beginning to supplant the RV-1D variant.

# LOCKHEED EC/MC/WC-130 HERCULES

**Manufacturer: Lockheed Aeronautical Systems Company, Georgia Division, USA.**
**Users: USA, Great Britain.**
**Role: Sigint, Command Control and Communications ($C^3$), $C^3$ countermeasures, covert infiltration, weather reconnaissance.**
**Data (EC-130E): Length 97ft 9in; wing span 132ft 7in; height 38ft 3in.**
**Powerplant: 4 × Allison T56-A-7 turboprops. Crew 12–16.**

The ubiquitous Hercules transport has been adapted to undertake numerous peripheral missions since the first of the breed flew on 7 April 1955. Among the more significant marks are the hotch-potch fleet of special mission aircraft assigned to various limbs of the USAF, including: twenty AC-130A/H 'Spectre' gunships assigned to Eglin Auxiliary bases Hurlburt and Duke Field, Florida (due to be supplemented by twelve new AC-130Us, which will oust the aged 'A' models); seven EC-130E/H 'Comfy Levi' command and control platforms stationed at Keesler AFB, Mississippi; eight 'Volant Solo' EC-130Es which listen in on enemy transmissions and broadcast radio and TV propaganda, all of which serve with the Pennsylvania Air National Guard at Harrisburg; ten EC-130H 'Compass Call' Comint and communications-jamming aircraft split between Davis-Monthan AFB, Arizona, and Sembach AB, Germany; fourteen MC-130E 'Combat Talon' covert infiltration and reconnaissance aircraft assigned to Hurlburt, and on detachment to Rhein-Main, Germany, and Clark Field in the Philippines (being supplemented by two dozen MC-130H advanced versions); and eight glossy-grey WC-130E/H weather reconnaissance aircraft split between Keesler AFB, and Andersen AFB in Guam. A solitary RAF Hercules W.2, its nose fitted with a 'barber shop' sensing proboscis and its spine sporting the relocated mapping radar, serves as a meteorological research tool. Perhaps the prettiest Hercules flying are the 23 HC-130Hs of the US Coast Guard, which fly on maritime rescue and patrol missions.

Many of these aircraft, such as the AC-130, feature low light-level and FLIR sensors which have been ably employed in both war and peace, performing a multitude of tasks which have ranged from locating the survivors of air and sea disasters to the surreptitious evaluation of enemy forces in Vietnam and Central America. Others, such as the MC-130E, have been employed in covert Photint of the Eastern Bloc; this mark can carry an internal reconnaissance module, complete with its own photo-processing and interpretation facility, capable of autonomous operations at austere locations for up to two weeks. Elint data are garnered by the more esoteric EC-130E/H 'Volant Solo' and 'Compass Call' versions, which now fly in subdued grey camouflage paint.

▲ The 193rd Special Operations Group, Pennsylvania Air National Guard, operates eight EC-130E/H 'Volant Solo' (originally 'Coronet Solo II') Hercules in the Comint and propaganda roles. [*USAF via Roger Chesneau*]

▲▶ The DC-130A/E 'Combat Angel' Hercules served as mothership for Teledyne Ryan Aeronautical Model 147 AQM-34 and for 'stealthy' AQM-91 'Compass Arrow' UAVs during the Vietnam war. Today the survivors are used for evaluating over-the-horizon radar defences. [*Teledyne Ryan Aeronautical*]

▶ Ten EC-130H 'Compass Call' command, control & communications countermeasures and Comint aircraft serve with the 41st and 43rd Electronic Combat squadrons based at Sembach, Germany, and Davis-Monthan, Arizona. The Stateside force is scheduled to move to Bergstrom in Texas.

# LOCKHEED EP/P-3 ORION

**Manufacturer: Lockheed Aeronautical Systems Company, California, USA. Production to shift to the Marietta, Georgia Division.**
**Users: USA, Australia, Canada, Iran, Japan, Netherlands, New Zealand, Norway, Portugal, Spain, South Korea.**
**Role: Maritime patrol, ASW, anti-shipping, Sigint.**
**Data (EP-3E): Length 116ft 10in; wing span 99ft 8in; height 33ft 8½in.**
**Powerplant: 4 × Allison T56-A-15 turboprops. Crew 10.**

▲▶ Twelve Elint EP-3E Orions serve with the US Navy's Fleet air reconnaissance countermeasures squadrons VQ-1 at NAS Agana, Guam, and VQ-2 at NAS Rota, Spain. [*Lockheed Aeronautical Systems Company*]

The P-3A through 'F series of maritime patrol aircraft is used by more air arms than any other aircraft in its class. The father of all Orions first flew on 24 November 1959, derived from the civil Electra airliner. Thirty-two years later, the Orion remains in production, having recently been given a reprieve following the announcement that South Korea is to purchase eight P-3Cs. Equipped with AN/ARS-3 sonobuoys, AN/APS-115 overwater radar and MAD, the Orion equips no fewer than 26 active and fourteen reserve patrol squadrons of the US Navy, along with the following major foreign customers: Australia (20 P-3Cs), Canada (eighteen of the similar CP-140 Aurora, which combines the avionics of the P-3C Orion and S-3A Viking), Iran (six P-3Es, of which only two or three remain operational), Japan (100 hundred P-3C), Netherlands (thirteen P-3C), New Zealand (six P-3Bs), Norway (seven P-3B), Portugal (six ex-Australian P-3Bs), and Spain (seven P-3As). Modernization of the force continues. The follow-on P-7 version was cancelled in July 1990. Instead, the US Navy is working on a P-3H programme that would employ the current 'Update IV' package and new engines.

The specialized Elint model was evolved during 1969 when two aircraft (BuNos 149669 and 149678) were reconfigured to EP-3B standard. Subsequently updated to EP-3E standard and joined by an additional ten aircraft between 1971 and 1975, the twelve machines were split between two Fleet air reconnaissance countermeasures squadrons, VQ-1 at NAS Agana, Guam, and VQ-2 at NAS Rota, Spain. The equipment fit is extensive, and includes a United Technologies Laboratory AN/ALQ-110 Elint radar plotter, E-Systems AN/ALD-8 radio direction finder, Argo AN/ALR-52 frequency-measuring receivers and GTE-Sylvania AN/ALR-60 radio communications listening devices. The EP-3E's chief task is to monitor Soviet ships' radar and communications transmitters to assist the US Navy in developing its own search systems and in preparing counter-measures to defeat Soviet defences.

Additional Orions are employed in the comparatively peaceful role of monitoring shipping on behalf of the US Customs service. The Federal organization received the first of two P-3 AEW Orions (equipped with the dorsal AN/APS-125 rotodome of the Grumman E-2C Hawkeye) on 17 June 1988, and these aircraft operate from NAS Corpus Christi, Texas.

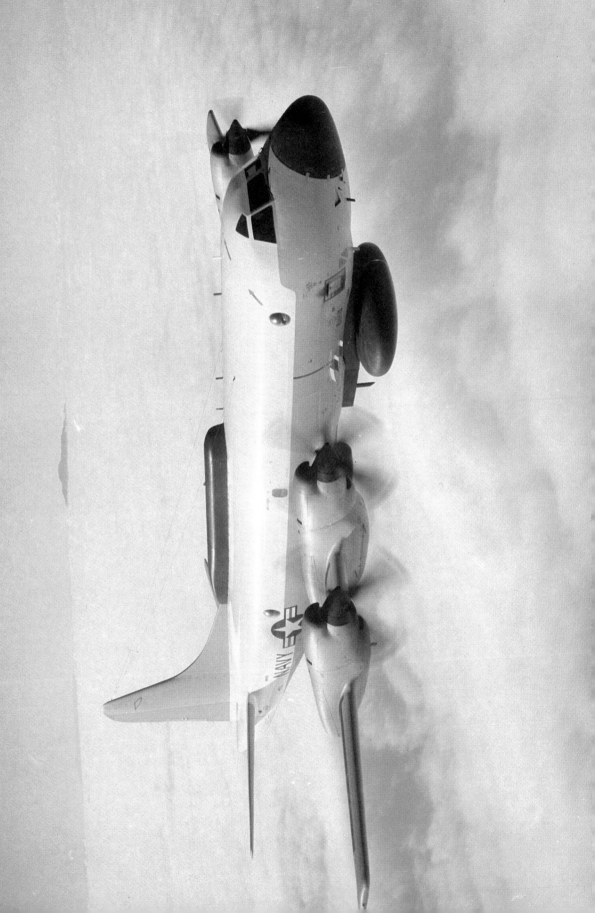

# LOCKHEED ES/S-3 VIKING

**Manufacturer: Lockheed Aeronautical Systems Company, California Division, USA.**
**User: US Navy.**
**Role: ASW, Sigint.**
**Data (S-3B): Length 53ft 4in; wing span 68ft 8in; height 22ft 9in.**
**Powerplant: 2 × General Electric TF34-2 turbofans. Crew 4.**

▲A pretty S-3A Viking of VS-28 'Gamblers', its wings folding up at the close of a training sortie. [Mil-Slides]

▶Viking BuNo 157993 served as aerodynamic trials machine for the ES-3A Sigint fit, being applied to sixteen aircraft which will eventually operate with reconnaissance countermeasures squadrons VQ-5 and VQ-6. [Lockheed Aeronautical Systems Company]

The first of eight pudgy YS-3A development carrier-borne sub-hunters flew on 21 January 1972. Production through 1978 totalled 187 S-3As, equipping eleven operational squadrons and one Fleet Replacement training unit, VS-41 'Shamrocks' based at NAS North Island, California. The first cruise was made by VS-21 'Fighting Redtails' aboard the USS *John F. Kennedy* during July 1975.

Originally designed with a 13,000-hour life (since amended upwards by 30 per cent), the S-3A Viking has plenty of unexpired fatigue life left and the surviving force is now being updated to S-3B standard. New equipment includes the Loral AN/ALR-76 ESM, AN/APS-137 ISAR (inverted synthetic aperture radar), QR-263 FLIR, and an enhanced MAD, managed by a crew of two pilots and two electronics specialists.

A further sixteen airframes are being adapted to the ES-3A Sigint and Battle Group Passive Horizon Extension System (BGPHES) roles. The testbed (BuNo 157993) first flew in September 1989 and the production aircraft will carry equipment almost identical to that of the EP-3E Orion, but providing a seagoing capability. New Link 11 UHF/HF communications equipment and three AYK-14 mission computers form part of the new kit, which is manifested as three new radomes and 35 blade antennae. The new ES-3As will form two eight-aircraft squadrons, VQ-5 and VQ-6, and these will deploy aboard carriers as two-plane detachments.

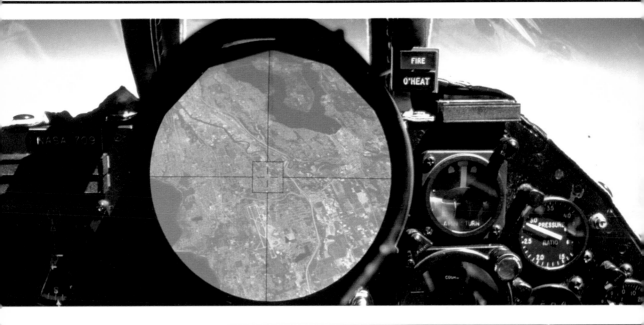

Manufacturer: Lockheed Aeronautical Systems Company, California Division, USA.
Users: NASA, USAF.
Role: Earth-resources monitoring, Photint and Sigint.
Data: Length 63ft; wing span 103ft; height 16ft 6in.
Powerplant: 1 × Pratt & Whitney J75-P-13B turbojet. Crew 1.

▲ A crisp driftsight view of Seattle-Tacoma (SEATAC) airport in Washington, photographed by NASA 'Dragon Lady' pilot Ronald W. Williams at a height of 65,000ft and an indicated airspeed of 120 knots. [*NASA*]

▶ On 17 and 18 April 1989 NASA U-2C 709 (formerly U-2H 56-6682) broke two world records in Classes C-1F/G previously held by a Gates Learjet 28, including an altitude of 73,700ft. Time to climb to 65,600ft (20,000 metres) was only 12min 13sec. The pilots concerned were Jerry Hoyt and Ron Williams. [*Lockheed Aeronautical Systems Company*]

Originally assigned the spurious prefix 'U' for Utility, Lockheed's high-flying U-2 series gained notoriety when one of its number, piloted by Francis Gary Powers, was brought down over the Soviet Union on May Day, 1960. The little 'spyplane', of which 53 were manufactured during the late 1950s, was nicknamed 'Dragon Lady' by those who flew her because of her unforgiving handling characteristics at altitude at the critical stall/buffet margin. This initial batch was phased out of service by 1980.

In the intervening years the U-2 evolved into its current, enlarged configuration, this offering much improved handling characteristics and a two-ton reconnaissance payload. Strategic Air Command and its clandestine partner the CIA took delivery of a dozen of the U-2R mark (serials 68-10329 to -10340) following its maiden flight on 28 August 1967 with Lockheed veteran William M. Parks at the controls. These aircraft served with distinction in South-East Asia, demonstrating a remarkable 98 per cent reliability. In the post-war years the survivors were consolidated under the 9th Strategic Reconnaissance Wing at Beale AFB, California, where they serve to this day. Working on ever-growing assignments, after a lull of eleven years the decision was made to reopen the production lines at Lockheed to make good attrition and to bolster the hard-pressed force.

The first in the new production batch took to the air on 1 August 1981, with Lockheed test pilot Ken Weir at the controls. The new build was designated Tactical Reconnaissance One to avoid the stigma attached to the old U-2 'skyplane' image, although production included the planned U-2R attrition replacemets (there exists no substantial differences between the two types, save for their operational equipment fit, which remains interchangeable by means of detachable 'superpods', noses and equipment pallets). Tail 80-1099, the last in the series, was delivered on 3 October 1989, bringing to an end a production run of 34 single-seaters and three twin-seat 'tubs', which joined the surviving batch of eight U-2Rs.

Today SAC operates two TR-1Bs and one U-2RT trainer, together with seventeen U-2R and 21 TR-1A operational variants which are split between the 9th SRW at Beale and

the 17th RW, based at RAF Alconbury in England. Some twenty forward operating locations are also in regular use, including the key bases Det 2 at Osan AB, South Korea, Det 3 at RAF Akrotiri, Cyprus, and Det 5 at Patrick AFB, Florida. Optional equipment includes the Hughes ASARS-2 ground-mapper, 'Senior Spear Phase IV' Sigint receiving kit (operating primarily in the Comint part of the spectrum, and manifested by a plethora of ventral blade antennae), and optical LOROPS, the latter being the chief province of the 'R' model. Most of these devices work in 'near real-time', and can be recorded simultaneously for detailed post-mission interpretation. For special long-range data-linking of urgent informtion, three machines (U-2Rs 68-10331, 80-1070 and -1071) sport distinctive E-Systems 'C-Span III' satellite dishes buried beneath large dorsal radomes.

In contrast to the SAC fleet of 'Dragon Ladies', painted in the radar- and light-attenuating matt 'Black Velvet' decor, NASA flies two glossy ER-2 (Earth Resources) machines from Moffett Field, California, on various peaceful assignments which range from land management survey and ozone sampling to pre-launch trials of satellite-based sensors. These wear the military serials 80-1063 (tail N706NA) and -1097 (tail N709NA) as a means of avoiding Federal fuel taxes and are regularly despatched across the world in pursuit of their various programmes, which are financed on an as-required basis by the Government, NASA, approved contractors and academic bodies.

Under a major modernization initiative, the 'Dragon Ladies' will be retrofitted with the modern General Electric F101-GE-F29 turbofan. This will extend the current 3,000nm range by 15 per cent, push the operational ceiling to 80,000ft, and overcome many of the woes associated with the aged and increasingly difficult to maintain J75 (originally poached from F-105 and F-106 fighters and adapted to the high-altitude cruise role). Automated ground-processing stations are also being procured further to speed the quality and 'timeliness' of the raw data-linked reconnaissance products. The first of these, installed for trials for late 1987 near Hahn AB, Germany, and allegedly since shifted nearer the Gulf region, is the semi-mobile Ford Aerospace Tactical Reconnaissance Exploitation Demonstration System (TREDS). It is to be superseded by the TRIGS information processing and data dissemination package, the first of which is to be buried underground at Gossberg Hill near Weuschheim, Germany, where it will help to keep an eye on Eastern Bloc forces. With these aids and updates, it is envisaged that the high aspect ratio 'birds' will continue to wheel in the upper skies for another twenty years, monitoring the global status quo.

◀▲ The TR-1A/U-2R is capable of carrying over tons of Sigint and Photi equipment. High-altitu cruise is made possible b the glider-like high aspe ratio wing, though the 'Dragon Lady' is anythir but a docile sailplane! Crews fly with the engines trimmed to ma cruise climb. Myths abo the machines gliding in the stratosphere to extend range are scoffe at by the crews. [USAF]

▲ Full-pressure suits are mandatory for all flight above 45,000ft. 'Dragor Lady' crews wear the David Clark Company S1030 pressure suit, also worn by former SR-71 crewmen and early Spac Shuttle pilots. [Lockhee Aeronautical Systems Company photo by Eric Schulzinger]

▶ Old and new in formation. NASA receiv two ER-2 Earth Resource aircraft from the second production batch of 37 'Dragon Ladies', and these replaced aged U-2 now on display at Ames and Robins AFB, Georgi the home aerodrome [Lockheed Aeronautical Systems Company]

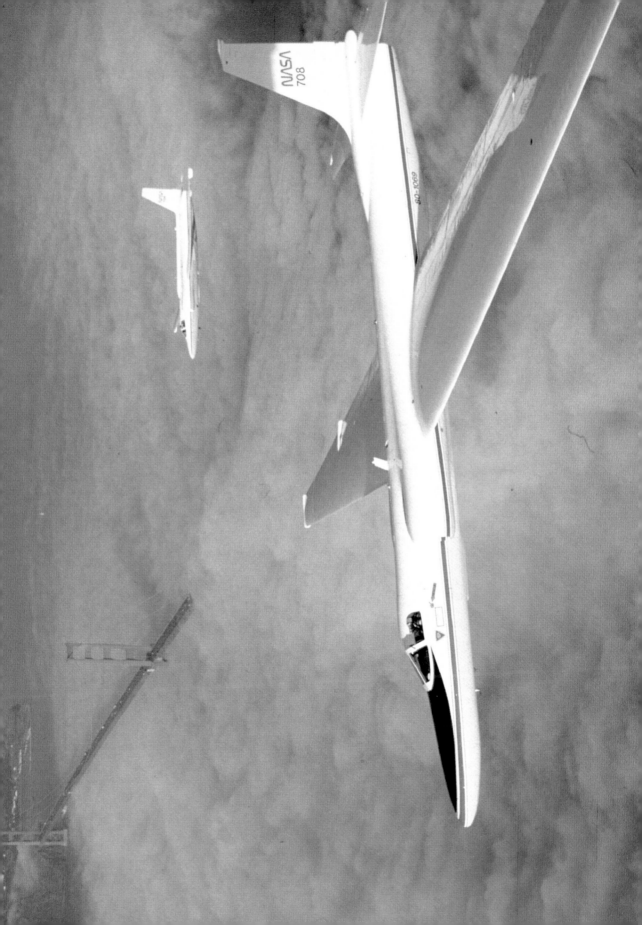

# LOCKHEED F-117A 'NIGHTHAWK'

**Manufacturer: Lockheed Aeronautical Systems Company, USA.**
**User: USAF.**
**Role: Night deep interdiction/reconnaissance.**
**Data: Length 65ft 11in; wing span 43ft 4in; height 12ft 5in.**
**Powerplant: 2 × General Electric F404-GE-F1D2 turbofans. Crew 1.**

Popularly known as the 'Stealth fighter', this remarkable product of the famed 'Skunk Works' serves exclusively with Tactical Air Command's 37th TFW, headquartered at Tonopah Test Range Airfield, Nevada. Making its maiden flight on 18 June 1981 with Hal Farley at the controls, production of the top-secret machine totalled 59 (tail numbers 785 through 843), the last of which was accepted on 12 July 1990. Although intended primarily to serve as a deep-strike bomber, the F-117A was conceived as the C-SIRS (Covert, In-weather Reconnaissance-Strike), and limited reconnaissance capability is possible by means of its two IDS sets, which are linked to a computer-modelled flight plan for accurate sensor cueing. It is alleged that its pilots can track targets with an accuracy of the order of one metre, and that such imagery can be recorded on an AVTR for post-mission analysis.

The F-117A first saw combat on the night of 20 December 1989 during Operation 'Just Cause', when two 'Bat Planes' struck pre-planned co-ordinates at Rio Hato, Panama, in support of US Rangers. More recently, on 20 August 1990, twenty selected aircraft from Colonel Alton C. Whitley's Wing deployed to Western Saudi Arabia as part of Operation 'Desert Shield'. The machine's extraordinary 'Stealth' features make it ideally suited to clandestine reconnaissance duties over Iraq, and aircraft have been noted flying with and without their radar reflectors fitted. As the reflectors are employed only during training sorties, it appears that passive intelligence-gathering missions, including limited Elint, are in fact being conducted. All 56 surviving aircraft ('tails' 785, 792 and 815 have been written off in crashes over Nevada and California) are gradually undergoing a major weapons systems improvement programme, which includes added provision for computer-enhanced reconnaissance and navigation.

▲ Nicknamed the 'Nighthawk' but also referred to as the 'Bat Plane' or 'Black Jet', the F-117A enjoyed a production run of 59 aircraft and there is talk of reopening the line at Palmdale, California. This machine is on approach to its first operational base, Tonopah Test Range Airfield, Nevada. [*Lockheed Aeronautical Systems Company photo by Eric Schulzinger and Denny Lombard*]

▶ The menacing F-117A 'Stealth' aircraft is designed to be almost invisible to hostile radars and infra-red search and tracking devices. The F-117A performs deep strike-reconnaissance, and the first of thirty-six machines were despatched to Western Saudi Arabia on 20 August 1990. [*Lockheed Aeronautical Systems Company photo by Eric Schulzinger and Denny Lombard*]

# LOCKHEED SR-71 'HABU'

**Manufacturer: Lockheed Aeronautical Systems Company, USA.**
**Users: USAF (storage) and NASA.   Role: Strategic reconnaissance/high-altitude research.**
**Data: Length 107ft; wing span 55ft 7in; height 18ft 6in.**
**Powerplant: 2 × Pratt & Whitney J58 (JT11D-20B) continuous-bleed afterburning turbo-ramjets. Crew 2.**

The most famous of all Lockheed's renowned 'Blackbirds', the Mach 3+ SR-71 was until very recently the world's fastest and highest-flying reconnaissance aircraft, capable of mapping up to 100,000 square miles of territory an hour using a variety of LOROPs and the Loral (formerly Goodyear Aerospace) ASARS-1 synthetic aperture radar contained in its snakelike forebody and interchangeable noses.

The first aircraft in the 'Skunk Works' production batch of 32 aircraft (including 29 'A' models, two 'B' model trainers, and a hybrid trainer built from spares and salvaged parts designated the 'C', but more popularly known as the 'bastard') flew on 22 December 1964 with test pilot Robert J. Gilliland at the controls. As part of the 'Senior Crown' programme, the initial cadre of crews was formed at Beale AFB, California, on 1 January 1965, under the auspices of the 4200th SRW. The first aircraft checked-in 53 weeks later and the unit became operational as the 9th SRW on 22 June 1966 under the command of Lieutenant Colonel Douglas T. Nelson. Flying operational sorties over North Vietnam and Korea, Cuba and the Middle East, and establishing a semi-permanent forward-operating presence at Kadena AB, Okinawa (Det 1) and RAF Mildenhall, England (Det 4), the type drew hostile fire from just over 1,000 surfarce-to-air missiles, *without loss*. Its other accomplishments included absolute world records for altitude in sustained level flight (set at 85,068.997ft on 28 July 1976), speed over a straight course (2,193.167mph, also on 28 July), and record-breaking excursions across the United States and Atlantic.

The SR-71's staggering operating costs, which climaxed at $40 million per aircraft annually, eventually signed its death knell. Although the aircraft is capable of performing in hours a task that still requires several orbits over a period of days from a satellite, the latter were deemed more cost-effective and during January 1990 the last of ten operational 'Habus' was removed from active service. Monitoring shipping on behalf of the US Navy formed some 90 per cent of its assignments during the latter years, and this 'ill use' prompted the sudden withdrawal of operating funds.

▲ 'Like a snake swallowing three mice' was how the inimitable Lockheed designer Clarence 'Kelly' Johnson described his masterpiece. Mr Johnson died on 21 December 1990, eleven months afte the SR-71 fleet was retired from active duty. His U-2Rs still fly today, as do a host of other Lockheed reconnaissance types. [*Lockheed Aeronautical Systems Company*]

▶ An SR-71 'Habu' traverses northern California following an AAR top-up. The glamorous fleet of ten operational aircraft (additional machines were stored and rotated through Palmdale for deep maintenance) held down a worldwide reconnaissance commitment under the 9th SRW and its detachment bases in England and Japan. [*Lockheed Aeronautical Systems Company*]

# McDONNELL DOUGLAS RF-4 'PHOTO PHANTOM'

**Manufacturer:** McDonnell Aircraft (McAir), USA.
**Users:** USAF, USMC, Germany, Greece, Iran, Israel, Japan, Spain and Turkey.
**Role:** Tactical recce/ELINT.
**Data:** Length 62ft 10¾in; wing span 38ft 4¾in; height 16ft 6in.
**Powerplant:** 2 × J79-GE-15 (RF-4C) or J79-GE-17 (RF-4E/EJ) afterburning turbojets. Crew 2.

Created as a major derivative from McAir's famous 'Fox-Four' do-it-all Phantom fighter, the (predominantly) unarmed 'Photo Phantom' first flew on 8 August 1963 when YRF-4C 62-12200 took off from Lambert Field, Missouri, with Bill Ross at the controls. Production orders eventually totalled 505 RF-4Cs for the USAF (of which four, and then a further eight, were supplied to Spain's Ejercito del Aire); 46 RF-4Bs for the USMC (retired during August 1990); and a total of 162 higher-performance RF-4E/EJs for Germany's Luftwaffe (88), Greece's Elliniki Aeroporia (8), Iran's pre-revolutionary Imperial Air Force (16), Israel's Cheyl Ha'Avir (15), Japan's Air Self-Defence Force (14), and Turkey's Turk Hava Kuvvetleri (8). Some 400 survivors remain in front-line service across the globe.

Equipment fits differ slightly according to customer and day-to-day operational requirements, while numerous updates have taken place over the years. Cameras typically embrace two CAI KS-87 oblique framing cameras, and KA-55/56 panoramic cameras, backed by an AN/AAS-18 or newer AN/AAD-5 IRLS and AN/APQ-102 SLAR.

Specialist equipment includes a number of dedicated Elint analyzers: in addition to an unspecified number of devices supplied by E-Systems to Germany, 23 Litton-Amecom AN/ALQ-125 Tactical Electromagnetic Receivers (TEREC) have been retrofitted into USAF RF-4Cs, capable of mapping radar defences in near real-time. Other specialist items of note include the Loral AN/UPD-4 SAR and its 'timely' derivatives, including the AN/UPD-8 which equips twenty USAF machines, and the AN/UPD-6 fitted to Luftwaffe aircraft. This can map tracts of ground at stand-off ranges of up to 50nm and relays the imagery via data-link over distances of up to 200nm. The Loral SARs provide true all-weather capability. 'Photo Phantoms' were blooded during the Vietnam War, where four RF-4Bs and 84 RF-4Cs were lost to all causes. Israel's RF-4Es have similarly been embroiled in hostilities over the Sinai Desert, where they have inadvertently acted as bait for Arab MiG-25 'Foxbats', the latter being despatched by marauding F-15 Eagles. More recently, the 117th TRW, Alabama Air National Guard, has been committed to Saudi Arabia. The unit possesses two aircraft equipped with CAI KS-127B 66in focal length LOROP cameras which can generate photographs featuring 1–2ft resolution when 'shot' at oblique ranges of up to 25nm! The clear desert skies are ideally suited to such devices, and similar sensors, including the General Dynamics HIAC-1, are fitted to two survivors of three specially converted Israeli F-4E(S) machines, alongside a small number of 'stock' Greek and Turkish RF-4Es.

▲ The 117th TRW, Alabama Air National Guard, has two RF-4Cs equipped with KS-172B LOROPS. Sadly, 64-044 pictured here was an early 'Desert Shield' casualty. On 8 September 1990 it crashed in the United Arab Emirates while on a daytime training mission. [*David Robinson*]

▲▶ Japan bought fourteen RF-4EJs from McAir and these were delivered between November 1974 and June 1975. The machines are operated by 501 Hikotai at Hyakuri Air Base. They are to be joined by seventeen F-4EJ fighters, shortly to be converted to RF-4 standard with a Thomson-CSF Raphael SLAR. [*Mil-Slides*]

▶ Quick-release hatches support the RF-4E's Photint gear, comprising KS-87 forward/oblique/vertical framing and KA-55 and -56 panoramic cameras. IRLS is fitted under the navigator's seat, aft of the nosegear well.

**Manufacturer:** McDonnell Aircraft (McAir), USA.
**User:** USAF.
**Role:** Defence-suppression, Elint.
**Data:** Length 63ft; wing span 38ft 4¾in; height 16ft 6in.
**Powerplant:** 2 × General Electric J79-GE-17C-G afterburning turbojets. Crew 2.

▲ A rare uncensored glimpse of the F-4G 'Weasel's' rear cockpit, complete with panoramic and homing indicators, designed to display the radar threats picked up by the aircraft's AN/APR-38A HAWC. *[John J. Harty]*

Converted from Fiscal 1969 F-4E stocks in two separate production batches (116 aircraft between 1977 and 1981, and an additional eighteen machines during 1987) the F-4G 'Advanced Wild Weasel V' forms the leading edge of the USAF's suppression of enemy defences (SEAD) forces. Equipped with the sensitive radar-sniffing AN/APR-38 homing and warning computer matched to in-flight tunable anti-radar missiles, along with the usual gamut of cluster and 'smart' bombs, the 'Weasel's' primary mission is to flush out and then destroy, or 'quieten', all enemy anti-aircraft systems opposing a friendly strike force. In the passive mode as a secondary role, the AN/APR-38A becomes a highly effective Elint tool, and data may be recorded on tape for post-mission analysis. Indeed, Phase 1 of the Performance Update Programme, Unisys's WASP (Weasel Attack Signal Processor), was introduced in 1987 and this has increased computer memory by a factor of eight and speeded radar analysis seven-fold. The new package is designated AN/APR-47 and has

▲F-4G hunter-killer 'Wild Weasels' on the wing with Texas Instruments AGM-88 HARM radar-zapping missiles. The force is based at George AFB, California, under the 35th TFW and at Spangdahlem AB, Germany, with the 52nd TFW. [USAF]

demonstrated excellent Elint performance, particularly in high-threat areas where the unarmed 'Ferrets' (see Boeing EC/RC-135 and McDonnell Douglas RF-4 'Photo Phantom') dare not venture.

During the force's zenith there were three Wings of F-4Gs and their 'hunter-killer' companions deployed worldwide: one at Spangdahlem, Germany, another at Clark Field in the Philippines, and the nucleus of the force at George AFB, California – 'Home of the Wild Weasels'. Owing to tightening budget purse strings and the increasing age of the aircraft (the majority of the original F-4E airframes were built during 1970, and have each clocked up several thousand hours), the fleet is being gradually wound down. Spangdahlem continues to operate two dozen F-4Gs for the time being, but the Pacific-based contingent has been phased out and George's aircraft have shrunk to two squadrons: the training unit, the 562nd TFTS 'Weasels'; and the 561st TFS 'Black Knights'. Four dozen of these aircraft, wearing their distinctive 'WW' tail codes but stripped of individual unit markings, were deployed to Saudi Arabia between August and December 1990, in two waves. Complete phase-out is scheduled to take place by 1995, and may be brought forward. There is no replacement in the offing, and the mission will eventually pass to 'vanilla' fighters equipped with improved threat-warning systems.

# MiG-21 'FISHBED'

**Manufacturer: Mikoyan-Guryevich Bureau, USSR.**
**Users: USSR, Czechoslovakia, Egypt, Poland.**
**Data (MiG-21RF): Length 51ft 8½in; wing span 23ft 5½in; height 14ft 9in.**
**Powerplant: 1 × Tumanski R-13-300 afterburning turbojet. Crew 1.**

▲MiG-21M of TAS 47 taxies replete with recce pod at its home drome Preschen, located near the Polish border.
[*Christian Gerard*]

A superb point-interceptor for its day, the MiG-21 has been produced in sixteen major versions over the past 30 years, two of which – the MiG-21R (a derivative of the 'Fishbed-J') and MiG-21-RF ('Fishbed-H') – were built specifically for reconnaissance duties with the Warsaw Pact and its allies. Both these types introduced a semi-permanent ventral reconnaissance pack in lieu of the traditional 'strap-on' GSh-23 guns, combining standard optical devices and IRLS.

Details remain sketchy owing to the gradual erosion of the force. Confirmed operators include the USSR, with some 50 aircraft in service at home and on 'loan' to Afghanistan; Czechoslovakia, with 40 'RFs divided between two Regiments; Poland, with 35 'RFs; and Egypt. Pods, which can be speedily strapped to the later generation MiG-23/27 'Floggers' and the newer MiG-29 'Fulcrum', are gaining greater prominence.

▲In its day the Foxbat was the fastest and highest flying reconnaissance aircraft. [*Hans-Heiri Stapfer*]

**Manufacturer: Mikoyan-Guryevich Bureau, USSR.**
**Users: USSR, India, Libya.**
**Role: High-altitude strategic reconnaissance.**
**Data: Length 74ft 6in; wing span 46ft; height 16ft 6in.**
**Powerplant: 2 × Tumanski R-31 afterburning turbojets. Crew 1.**

Derived from the record-breaking Ye-26 demonstrator which grew into the 40-ton MiG-25 interceptor (NATO codename 'Foxbat'), some 205 of the MiG-25R reconnaissance version were built between 1969 and around 1977 in two distinct submodels: the 'Bravo', equipped with SLAR, one vertical and four oblique long-range cameras; and the 'Delta', which is rigged with the SLAR and an array of Elint receivers. Both types are equipped with 'Jaybird' radar and a vertical view-finder.

Some 160 aircraft were ordered into production for the Soviet Frontal Aviation (many of which have allegedly since been withdrawn), and on detachment with 'customer' forces such as Algeria and Vietnam (four 'Bs' each), flown by Soviet pilots. True exports include eight 'Bs' to India in 1982, these being operated by Special Flight of No 106 Squadron, five 'B/Ds' to Libya, and an unspecified number to Iraq (which operates at least ten of the MiG-25 interceptor version). Possessing a dash speed in the region of Mach 3.2 at 88,500ft, the 'Foxbat' is unquestionably the present ruler of the upper skies in terms of both speed and altitude, although its days are numbered. In a philosophy mirroring that of the United States, the bullet-beating aircraft is being phased out in favour of high-altitude, high-aspect-ratio cruise aircraft such as the new Molniya M-17 'Mystic', a twin-boomed Russian 'Dragon Lady'.

# NORTHROP RF-5E TIGEREYE

**Manufacturer:** Northrop, USA.
**Users:** Malaysia, Saudi Arabia and Thailand.
**Role:** Tactical and low-threat strategic reconnaissance.
**Data:** Length 48ft; wing span 26ft 8in; height 13ft 4in.
**Powerplant:** 2 × General Electric J85-GE-21B afterburning turbojets. Crew 1.

▲The sharklike Northrop RF-5E Tigereye dormant at Edwards AFB, California. This cost-effective little beast equips the air arms of Malaysia, Saudi Arabia and Thailand, and can be fitted with one of three strap-on reconnaissance packages. [*Frank B. Mormillo*]

One of the most cost-effective reconnaissance jets operational, Northrop's petite RF-5E is a direct descendant of the successful RF/F-5 and T-38 series (flown by no fewer than 31 countries). The RF-5E Tigereye with its distinctive 'shark nose' reconnaissance modifications first flew at Edwards AFB, California, on 29 January 1979.

Replacing the X-Band radar and pair of M39 20mm cannon in the 'shark nose' is a forward-facing KS-87D1 framing camera, behind which one of three pallets may be fitted: the low/medium-altitude module featuring KA-56E and -95B panoramic cameras plus Texas Instruments RS-710E IRLS; the medium/high-altitude KA-56E plus KA-93B6 panoramic camera package; or the high-altitude/long-range oblique pallet fitted with 66in KS-172B or -174A LOROPS. Sold chiefly under the foreign Military Assistance Programme, the launch customer was Malaysia, which received two machines (coded FM2201 and FM2202). These are operated by No 12 Squadron based at Butterworth. Saudi Arabia received ten Tigereyes under the 'Peace Hawk' programme (at least one of which wears overall black camouflage for night-time work), distributed between the Tiger bases at Dhahran, Khamis Mushayt and Taif. The biggest user is Thailand, which flies two dozen aircraft under the authority of the 1st Air Wing headquartered at Nakhom Ratchisima, whose primary job is to keep an ever-vigilant eye on its belligerent neighbour Vietnam.

# PANAVIA TORNADO GR.1A/ECR

The RAF's No 2 Squadron was the first to quip with Tornado GR.1As, beginning in January 1989. The distinctive SLIR infra-red sensors replaced the Mauser cannon. [*Tim Laming*]

No 13 Squadron at RAF Honington was the second Tornado GR.1A reconnaissance unit to form. The machines are equipped with SLIRs, IRLS and six video recorders, for round-the-clock reconnaissance capability. [*Tim Laming*]

**Manufacturer: Panavia Anglo-German-Italian consortium.**
**Users: RAF, Germany.**
**Role: Tactical reconnaissance, strike, Elint and defence-suppression.**
**Data (ECR): Length 54ft 10¼in; wing span, fully extended (at 25deg) 45ft 7½in, fully swept (at 67deg) 28ft 2¼in; height 19ft 6¼in.**
**Powerplant: 2 × RB.199 Mk 105 augmented turbofans, with thrust-reversing. Crew 2.**

Making its maiden flight on 14 August 1974 and first entering service with the Trinational Tornado Training Establishment at RAF Cottesmore, which was commissioned on 29 January 1981, the Tornado IDS (interdictor-strike) remains in production and equips the air forces of Britain (220 for the RAF), Germany (212 for the Luftwaffe and 112 for the Marineflieger), Italy (100 for the Aeronautica Militare Italiana) and Saudi Arabia (60).

For dedicated reconnaissance duties, the RAF has received two dozen machines which have been modified to GR.1A configuration. In contrast to the reconnaissance Jaguar (see SEPECAT Jaguar GR.1A) which it is gradually replacing, the Tornado fit is internal, and includes two sideways-looking infra-red sensors (which replaced the two Mauser cannon) and an IRLS, which project the imagery in the cockpit for in-flight editing. The GR.1A boasts some six AVTRs (known simply at VCRs in RAF parlance), while radar ground maps can also be recorded. All data are annotated with the assistance of the INS and navcomputer, which is fed a modelled flight-plan prior to take-off by means of the Tornado's CPGS (Cassette Preparation Ground Station). The first unit to equip was No 2 Squadron based at RAF Laarbruch, Germany, in January 1989, since followed by No 13 Squadron at RAF Honington, England.

Another key 'spyplane' variant of the Tornado is the Electronic Combat Reconnaissance (ECR) model, the prototype of which (German serial 9806) first flew on 18 August 1988. Italy's order for sixteen machines has since been cancelled, but Germany is forging ahead with a production run of 35 aircraft, equipped with Honeywell-Sondertechnik IRLS, FLIR, and a full complement of Texas Instruments AGM-88 HARM anti-radar missiles matched to the new TI/Deutschland GmbH Emitter Location System, which picks up key information on SAM, AAA and fighter threats. Beginning in May 1991, the aircraft will equip Jagdbombergeschwader 3 (JBG 32) at Lechfeld, the cutting edge, and JBG 38 at Jever, the training unit with a shadow operational tasking. Additional reconnaissance duties are at present undertaken by the Marineflieger's (Germany Navy) No 2 Gruppe, which operates a handful of standard strike Tornadoes equipped with strap-on recce pods.

# ROCKWELL INTERNATIONAL OV-10D BRONCO

**Manufacturer:** North American Rockwell International, USA.
**Users:** USA, Germany, Morocco, Indonesia, Thailand and Venezuela.
**Role:** Forward Air Control, Counter-Insurgency.
**Data (OV-10D):** Length 44ft; wing span 40ft; height 15ft 2in.
**Powerplant:** 2 × Garrett T76-G-420/421 counter-rotating turboprops. Crew 2.

▲Seventeen OV-10D NOS Broncos were converted for the US Marines, and these serve with VMQ-1 at New River MCAS, North Carolina, on forward air control and observation duties, equipped with FLIR and a laser gun. [*Mil-Slides*]

Spawned as the North American 300 in the early 1960s and given a boost by the need for a modern FAC and COIN (Counter-Insurgency) machine for duties in Vietnam, the 'Buckin' Bronco' first flew on 16 July 1965 and made its combat debut during June 1968. Initial production totalled 157 for the USAF and 114 for the USMC. Overseas customers included Morocco (which received six surplus USAF aircraft), and Germany (sixteen OV-10B/BZs), Indonesia (sixteen OV-10Fs), Thailand (forty OV-10Cs), and Venezuela (sixteen OV-10Es).

Most of the American machines are being gradually phased out in favour of the OA-10A 'Warthog FAC' (see Fairchild Republic OA-10A), with the exception of twelve (of seventeen) OV-10D-NOS (Night Observation Surveillance) aircraft operated by the US Marines under VMQ-1 at New River MCAS, North Carolina. Converted to the NOS role from OV-10A airframes beginning in 1979, the aircraft are equipped with an AN/AAS-37 laser target designator and FLIR turret, auto-video tracker, and typically fly in the armed surveillance role, toting an M197 three-barrel 20mm gun with 1,500 rounds and pods packing 2.75in FFAR and 4in rockets.

Denmark's Kongelige Danske Flyvevaaben received twenty RF 35 Draken reconnaissance aircraft and a further eleven dual-capable recce-trainer TF 35s. One of the latter is seen here, complete with crammed cockpit and ESK 729 badge on the nose.

**Manufacturer:** Saab-Scania, Sweden.
**Users:** Sweden, Denmark.
**Role:** Tactical reconnaissance.
**Data (RF 35):** Length 50ft 4⅓in; wing span 30ft 10in; height 12ft 9in.
**Powerplant:** 1 × Volvo Flygmotor RM6C afterburning turbojet. Crew 1.

Entering service as a fighter in March 1960, the remarkable cranked-delta fighter soon evolved into the S 35E reconnaissance model for service with the Svenska Flygvapen (Swedish Air Force). Now all but retired in its country of origin, the biggest user is Denmark which ordered some 46 aircraft in 1968–69. These included 20 of the F 35 interceptor version, 20 RF 35 Photint reconnaissance models and six dual-capable trainer-recce TF 35s (joined by five more during 1973). In addition to their onboard optical sensors, the aircraft are equipped to carry Texas Instruments IRLS mounted in an FFV 'Red Baron' pod.

Today, some eighteen RF 35s and five TF 35s remain in service with Eskadrille 729 stationed at Karup, Denmark. Thirteen of these aircraft will receive a digital upgrade to keep them viable beyond 1995.

# SAAB SF/SH 37 VIGGEN

**Manufacturer: Saab-Scania, Sweden.**
**User: Sweden.**
**Role: Tactical and maritime reconnaissance, strike.**
**Data: Length 53ft 5¾in; wing span 34ft 9⅓in; height 19ft ⅓in.**
**Powerplant: 1 × Volvo Flygmotor RM8A (P&WA licence-built JT8D-22 adaptation)**
**afterburning turbojet, with thrust-reversing. Crew 1.**

▲The SF 37 Viggen first flew on 21 May 1973 and a total of 26 were procured for the Swedish Air Force, together with 26 SH 37 maritime surveillance models. The complex splinter camouflage is unique to the Viggen.

The SF 37 and SH 37 reconnaissance marks of the radical-looking Viggen are direct descendants of the Saab AJ 37 attack model, the SH 37 maritime surveillance type retaining a modified Ericsson PS-37/A attack radar and standard radome, while the dedicated Photint SF 37 was given a new 'chisel' nose containing optical sensors. Both types flew for the first time in 1973, the SF 37 on 21 May and the SH 37 on 10 December.

Twenty-six of each type were manufactured for the Svenska Flygvapen and these have been pooled into a composite force which equips three surveillance Wings: 'Bravala' Flygflottilj 13 (F 13 for short), based at Bravalla, which converted to one squadron of Viggens during 1976; 'Blenkinge' F 17, which operates two squadrons from Ronneby, and converted to the type during 1977; and 'Norrbottens' F 21, which has operated the two types at Lulea-Kallax since 1979.

Both models employ ventral FFV 'Red Baron' night-time reconnaissance pods (equipped with Texas Instruments RS-710 IRLS), or the larger 'Green Baron', fitted with the same IRLS and a suite of forward-looking, split-vertical and panoramic cameras with focal lengths varying between 1.5in and 12in.

A 'Desert Pink' Jaguar
R.1A tucks up its gear
ver RAF Coltishall,
ound for Thumrayt in
man, and toting
xternal fuel and
Westinghouse
N/ALQ-101 ECM pod.
Royal Air Force]

**Manufacturer: SEPECAT Anglo-French consortium.**
**User: RAF.**
**Role: Tactical reconnaissance, strike.**
**Data: Length 55ft 2.6in; wing span 28ft 6in; height 16ft 0.5in.**
**Powerplant: 2 × Rolls-Royce Turbomeca Adour Mk 104 augmented turbofans. Crew 1.**

The reconnaissance Jaguar is a pod-equipped adaptation of the standard RAF GR.1, of which 165 were procured following the maiden flight of the first British example on 12 October 1969. The recce pod was custom-built by BAe's Weybridge division, and features BAe IRLS in the rear plus two rotating 'barrels' fitted with stabilized Vinten cameras, all linked to the aircraft's NAVWASS inertial nav and attack system. The aft drum houses two F95 Mk 10 oblique cameras (or more powerful F126 camera module), while the front portion is equipped with two oblique F95 Mk 10s sporting 1.5in as opposed to the more usual 3in versions, together with a forward-facing F95 Mk 7. All but the F126 sensor, which is employed at medium altitude, are optimized for low-level reconnaissance.

The first of two dozen machines to be assigned to reconnaissance operations was XZ101, which was issued to No 2 Squadron at RAF Laarbruch, Germany, in 1976. Also equipping with the aircraft was No 41 Squadron at RAF Coltishall, which soldiers on today as the last 'Jag Recce' unit; No 2 Squadron has since re-equipped with Tornadoes (see Panavia Tornado GR.1A). Operation 'Granby' has tasked a dozen 'desert pink' Jaguars to the troubled Persian Gulf. Led out by Wing Commander Jerry Connolly on 11 August, the force embraces four recce examples (XZ115, XZ355, XZ357 and XZ363) which are assigned to Thumrayt in Oman. Additional aircraft joined ranks during January. The aircraft operate in a 'swing-role' manner and the pods may be downloaded to permit the carriage of standard air-to-surface weapons.

# TUPOLEV Tu-95/142 'BEAR'

Manufacturer: **Tupolev Bureau, USSR.**
Users: **USSR, India.**
Role: **Long-range maritime patrol, Photint, Sigint.**
Data: **Length 155ft 10in; wing span 167ft 8in; height 39ft 9in.**
Powerplant: **4 × Kuznetsov NK-12MV counter-rotating turboprops. Crew 8–16 (with standby crew).**

▲A Tu-95 'Bear-D' keeps company with an intercepting Tornado F.3 from No 5 Squadron, RAF 'Bears' generate more 'scrambles' than any other type of intruder, as they poke and prod at th UK's air defences. [*Crown Copyright*]

This giant silver machine grossing 175 tons and boasting an unrefuelled endurance of 28 hours is undoubtedly the fastest propeller-driven aircraft operational, capable of cruising at 570mph at 25,000ft (Mach 0.82). From a gentle starting speed, it can out-accelerate most fighters sent up to intercept it, leaving the opposition way behind for up to a minute! Big and rugged, its crews now use the NATO codename 'Bear'. Remarkably, the aircraft first flew as long ago as 1954, and a considerable percentage of the original 300 aircraft remain active today, as conversions and other refurbishing work keeps the force viable. Low-rate production of attrition replacements – about a dozen aircraft annually – is also maintaining the force in good order.

The principal types in service today with the Soviet V-VS (Air Force) and AV-MF (Naval Aviation) include: the 'Bear-D' Elint model, first noted in August 1967, and the most numerous of all types, with 40 in service; the Tu-95 'Bear-E' equivalent, dedicated to Maritime Elint and Photint and lacking any attack capability, of which some ten remain active; the Tu-142 'Bear-F' anti-submarine warfare model, first identified in 1973, five of which have been supplied to India and which has seen production in numerous sub-variants; the 'Bear-G' nuclear missileer equiped with AS-4 'Kitchen' missiles; the 'Bear-H', first noted in 1984 and equipped with long-range AS-15 'Kent' cruise missiles; and the latest model, the 'Bear-J', first seen in 1986 and assigned to Comint and command & control functions.